REBEL WITHOUT A CLUE

A Way-Off Broadway Memoir

Steve Hrehovcik

With Illustrations by the Author

"*Rebel without a Clue* is an autobiographical mosaic that provides great chucks of wisdom mixed with healthy doses of wit and humility. There is a lot to relate to here, especially for those of us who could have made better decisions along the way, but came through it smiling in spite of ourselves."

> Thomas Handel, Executive Director, Channel 5, Community Television Network, Portland, Maine, Theater Director and Actor

"Steve Hrehovcik's *Rebel Without A Clue* gives the reader a glimpse at what is his long and winding road of self-discovery and self-worth. Behind all the trials, disappointments and missed opportunities he encounters along the way is a man who still can smile and be thankful for his wife of 52 years, three great kids and a grandchild. Really isn't that what life is all about? Family, memories and the continuing drive to be a better person. Well done Steve."

> Robert Baldacci, Principal, Baldacci Group

"Steve's memoir is an engaging, genuine, and insightful read. Each time he saw a dream fail, he got up and dreamed again. As one who loved the theater, perhaps Steve's greatest role in life was to not stand still, but to grow, evolve and ultimately give back."

Jean M. Flahive, Author of *Billy Boy* and *Railroad to the Moon*

"Steve Hrehovcik takes us with him as he wrestles with the conflicting desires that lead him across the country and into different worlds of experience. Time and again the magic of the theater calls him away from employment that could provide for self and family. His *Rebel* is honestly revealed in his telling of the struggle between the romantic and practical. He openly, and often with humor, shares with us the self-doubts and disappointments that result. The sincerity and humility with which he writes are the magic in this memoir as he searches for that 'Clue' and the ultimate solution."

David Morse, Author of *Harry & Maude Take It On* and *Julie's Climb*

"Ever vulnerable and sensitive, Steve Hrehovcik bravely shares his stories by focusing inward to unfolding awareness. With brilliant metaphor, he holds us captive to identify and find meaning in our own clues in life which is a gift. A moving memoir that is an act of discovery in its perseverance."

J. Nelson Garman, Founder of
The Power Triangle

"Everybody has a story. Steve Hrehovcik's story, recounted with humor and humility in his memoir *Rebel Without A Clue*, is a heroic journey through an ordinary life. An Army veteran, aspiring actor, husband and father, Hrehovcik tells an inspirational story about taking advantage of opportunities, overcoming challenges and always finding the silver lining.

A theater thread runs through his tale. Hrehovcik fell in love with theater as a youngster, studied acting in college and shaped many important decisions in his life around opportunities in local theater. The big break he dreamed about never materialized, but he never stopped looking and never stopped dreaming. The other theme of this memoir is overcoming disappointment and finding a way forward, with morals and dignity intact. Acting teaches humility, and Hrehovcik displays it with life-lesson flair.

Hrehovcik's successes lie closest to the hearth. He's always supported his family, and his commitment to his primary mission in life is evidenced in his 50-plus year marriage to Carol, who has much more than a supporting role in Hrehovcik's journey. As he writes, 'Perhaps the curtain hasn't lowered on my last act just yet.' Perhaps not. Stay tuned. The best is yet to come."

> Bob Keyes, Arts Writer, Portland Press Herald/Maine Sunday Telegram

"*Rebel Without A Clue* is a down-to-earth nostalgic story about a man and his dreams. It will surely bring a smile to your face."

Leo J. Maloney, Author of the Dan Morgan Thriller Series by Kensington Publishing

Steve Hrehovcik has written a personal memoir that is at once candid, charming, insightful, and inspirational. It is a wild and glorious romp through a life well-spent, if at times sadly-lived, one that demonstrates in spades the value of love, persistence, and resilience in the face of hardship, challenge, and change."

Richard Barringer, Emeritus Professor, Muskie School of Public Service, University of Southern Maine

CONTENTS

DEDICATION

For Carol ...

who knew so much, long before I got a clue,

and

Josh, Noah and Gillian ...

who triumphed, in spite of my rebellions.

x

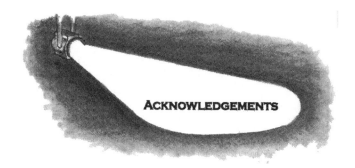

ACKNOWLEDGEMENTS

The gratitude I feel to all those who gave of their valuable time and good counsel for reading my memoir rises to the level of winning an Oscar. I never won an Oscar and, the odds are extreme I ever will. Yet, when I hear actors express their appreciation to all who made their precious moment possible in their glorious Hollywood limelight, I know the depth of their heartfelt thanks.

Elayne Star's eagle eye for commas, capitals and context saved considerable embarrassment for me. Paula Singer, who became a dear friend when we worked together on her own memoir, urged me to express myself with clarity and humor. David Morse, who provides leadership to our writers' group, caught mistakes my apparent dyslexia symptoms never noticed. Mort Mather, who knows a thing or three about good writing, pointed out overlooked grammatical blunders and redundant repetitions.

Ruth Story, whose memoir class I attended, wouldn't let me get away with overused expressions

and vague references. Other members in her class –
all excellent writers – helped just by allowing me to
listen to the way they crafted their stories, plus their
kindhearted critiques of my efforts.

Richard Barringer added important insights I
never considered, making my manuscript more
readable and fun.

For agreeing to write an introduction,
Ellsworth T. Rundlett III has my eternal thanks. You
should see his energetic performance of Elvis Presley.

Of course, the most important inspiration for
my writing is my wife Carol. Several people, after
reading early drafts of my memoir, canonized her as a
saint for putting up with my uncontrollable rebellions.
And I learned more from Josh, Noah and Gillian, our
three children, than they ever picked up from me.
They each turned out as remarkable people in spite of
my burdening them with my search for elusive clues.

For all their kindness and support, I am
grateful beyond words I can express. If I learned
anything from this journey, I realize the final words
I've expressed here in my memoir remain my
responsibility alone.

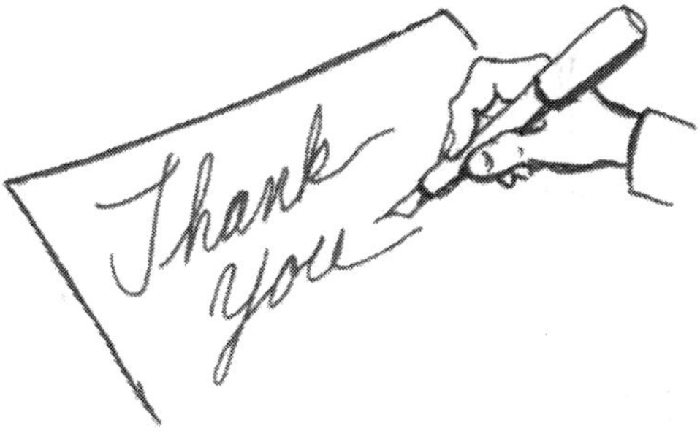
Thank you

FOREWORD

By Ellsworth T. Rundlett III

I first met Steve when we served on the board of directors of a community television network in Portland, Maine. He volunteered to organize an anniversary celebration for the station. I agreed to perform as Elvis Presley and a mutual admiration society resulted between us.

When I was asked to read this book and write a foreword I asked myself this question: "What is a rebel without a clue?" I must confess I would have difficulty trusting a clueless rebel. To me a clueless rebel brings to mind the image of a civil war soldier in a battlefield fighting soldiers from the north but not really knowing why. Steve is anything but a clueless rebel, though he certainly paints a picture of himself as a man who felt it was appropriate to question authority, tradition and the notion that one has to conform to rules simply because "that's the way it's always been done."

When one reads an autobiographical book they assume they will know the author much better after the last chapter. The reader obtains insight into how the author thinks, acts, and deals with the problems of life. At the end of this book you will know Steve Hrehovcik well. You will have no doubt about his integrity, his commitment to family, his work ethic, and his love of life.

I just finished the biography of the famous singer, Brenda Lee. She has become a rather close personal friend of mine in the past few years and when I finished the book I realized why I care for her so much. This woman not only had incredible talent, but also went through life working hard in her craft, was loyal to friends and family and gave back more than she took. Steve is no celebrity, but I had the same impression after reading this book. I now realize why I was so impressed with him as we sat through rather long and tedious board meetings. He is a person whose word you can count on. When he sets out to do something, he finishes. Thus, while many people tell their friends they are writing a book, most never do it. Steve did.

When you finish this book you will not necessarily find the secret to life, nor will you find the answers to the mysteries we all face every day. In fact, this book presents more questions than it does answers. It makes you think about your own life. You ask yourself, "How would I have dealt with this situation if it were me?"

In one chapter Steve talks about meeting a very famous celebrity. He was faced with a dilemma. He asks himself whether or not his life would have been far different had he acted a certain way. I faced a similar situation in the 1990s. I had come up with an idea for a motion picture about a lawyer who is appointed to represent all the whales of the world in the international court to oppose the killing of whales by various fishing industries in foreign countries. My older brother thought this was a fabulous idea and begged me to let him write the film treatment or summary for submission to motion picture producers. I let him do it, but in the final product he had changed some of my ideas substantially. He also decided that the only actor who could play the role of the lawyer was Jon Voight, famous for his role in *Midnight Cowboy* with Dustin Hoffman. What occurred shortly after I received the summary could only be described as one of the most amazing coincidences of my life.

Right after I received the film treatment I boarded a plane the next day to meet my family at Disney World in Florida. My plane changed in Washington, D.C. I put my things under a chair (you could do that back then) and went to the restroom. When I returned, a gentleman was sitting in the chair. It was Jon Voight. I could not believe my eyes, but I pulled out my briefcase and showed him the film treatment and the mention of his name. He, too, was amazed at this possible kismet meeting. He agreed to read the summary and we parted company with me giving him my business card.

A few weeks later he wrote me a letter saying he enjoyed the idea but did not like much of the plot, and thereby rejected any further involvement. I was devastated, and several years later while honeymooning with my wife in England, I drank too much wine at dinner and found myself crying my eyes out in our hotel room. When my wife asked what was wrong, I told her that I perhaps made the biggest mistake of my life by letting my brother write the script. Did I make a huge mistake? Was fate involved with this situation since God himself may have planted Jon Voight in that seat? I'll never know, and just like Steve, I can wonder until the cows come home, but it will make no difference.

I was also pleased to read that I am not the only man who has had a connection with a Hong Kong tailor. In my case, the three suits I bought would not have even fit my eight-year-old nephew, let alone a thirty-year-old man.

As Steve completes his story he lets us know what is really important in life – family. His wife, children, and his parents all played a role into making the man he is today. His expressions of praise, doubt, and love of his family will warm your heart and make you think of your own loved ones. It's a lesson in understanding the people who make up our lives.

In the end you will know him better. I know him better. I liked him before I read this book and I like him after reading it. In the end, I even felt better about myself knowing that another man has struggled with similar issues, similar challenges, and similar confrontations. How does the saying go? "Misery loves company." In this case we both learned that misery is part of life, but life has rewards. And, while he and I may have different opinions on how to handle various situations, I realize that I would, indeed, trust this *Rebel Without A Clue*. You will come to the same conclusion I did.

Steve Hrehovcik is anything but clueless.

Ellsworth Rundlett, known as Derry, is an attorney and author of a best-selling law treatise and a book, *Full Circle – A Father's Journey with a Transgender Child* co-authored with his daughter Nicole.

INTRODUCTION

"I hold it that a little rebellion now and then is a good thing ..."

Letter by *Thomas Jefferson to James Madison*

"How many apples fell on Newton's head before he took the hint?"

From *Comment* by *Robert Frost*

The clues surrounded me. They tapped me on the shoulder. They tugged at my sleeve. They stared me in the face. Clues, so obvious. Yet, I couldn't see them until much too late. Or if I did see them, they loomed like forlorn pieces of a puzzle that had no picture.

Looking back, I figured out why I was so dense. I couldn't see the clues because I received so many conflicting messages as a young boy.

One of my most penetrating influences came from my strict religious upbringing. Some of my earliest memories recall how my mother, a gentle and uncomplicated woman, taught me to pray. Of course, prayer can be powerful and uplifting. Except in my case I either misunderstood its meaning or I took it as a literal force.

When I was about four years old I remember praying for it to snow on my birthday, which is three days before Christmas. I figured if it snowed, Santa could come with presents. It seemed like a miracle, because it did snow. My mother told me God answered my prayer. I felt very powerful for a little boy. You can imagine my disappointment when my next prayer didn't have the same success. My tiny boy-heart broke.

I became bewildered even more when my mother told me God did answer my prayer. He said, "No." I struggled to understand this conflicting concept of an ungenerous God. At last I settled for the idea that I wasn't good enough to have my prayer answered.

This led to a lack of self-esteem that would color most of my growing years.

In a desperate attempt to make sense of my life I took those pieces of God's disappointment and jammed them together with other random pieces of disillusionment. I didn't have enough awareness to accomplish this life-view on a conscious level. It turned out as a haphazard, distorted image I twisted into some sort of reality.

Acting on this confused view I look back and see how I embraced the idea of a rebel. But at the time I did not have enough clues to even know what I rebelled against.

I didn't even rebel in a traditional sense. No wild clothes or hairstyles. No foul language or destructive behavior. Just the opposite. Much of my rebellion took on a passive role. I became a model of decorum. I was "good," often influenced by historic martyrs. I believe my parents sensed my inner torture, but I was beyond their ability to help.

Often, when overwhelmed, I withdrew into an imaginary world of fantasy. Other times, desperate for attention, I cried out for center stage and the spotlight. Such extreme behavior only confused everyone, especially me.

My only saving grace came from the satisfaction that somehow I survived and even managed to achieve some successes along the way.

I graduated from the University of Miami with a degree in Theater Arts with dreams of an acting career. That dream got postponed for two years while I served as an ROTC Army officer, most of it in South Korea. Thank God no one was shooting at anyone at the time.

What followed can only be described as a zigzag, checkered path. I discovered I had just enough drive and persistence to make a mark in professional theater, catalog copywriting, advertising, package design, sales and a host of desperate jobs I needed to provide for my wife and three children.

On the constant chase for a pot of gold at the end of a colorless rainbow, shifting career goals and taking serious financial and personal risks, I've come to a calm acceptance of my talents and limitations.

Today I find great satisfaction in that my family is doing well and I work as a freelance writer, artist and teacher.

But, oh how I wish those early years hadn't been so disastrous for me. Even more important, I shudder to think of how difficult I made it for other people. People who deserved better. My family, friends, people I worked with, even the people I met in a casual way.

I would have loved to have had someone explain what I was going through. Although, in keeping with my rebellious nature at the time, I doubt I would have heeded even the wisest counsel or advice.

Looking back on these exploits I'm amazed at how much I learned. That's why I write. In spite of the shattered dreams, bruised ego and broken promises, I discovered how to pick myself up and carry on.

There's a chance my "confessional" may shed light on your own journey. If so, my rebellion will have had some purpose.

Like mine were, the answers you seek may be hiding in plain sight. I could hope for no greater satisfaction than for the stories of my rebellion help you discover your clues.

Part I
Searching for Clues

"... You got to have a dream,
If you don't have a dream,
How you gonna have a dream come true?"

From *Lyrics "Happy Talk"* in *South Pacific*
Richard Rodgers and Oscar Hammerstein II

In 1954 when I was a sophomore in high school in Linden, New Jersey, I joined the dramatic club. The acting bug bit me early. That year we voted to see the long-running Broadway hit *South Pacific*. This would be my very first Broadway show, so it was all very exciting.

South Pacific had been breaking theater records with awards and captivating audiences since it opened in 1949. I knew most of the songs. "Some Enchanted Evening," "I'm Gonna Wash That Man Right Outa My Hair," "Bali Ha'i," "A Cockeyed Optimist" and "A Wonderful Guy" were all popular hits on the radio since the show opened. As a teenager dealing with coming-of-age issues the one song I recalled with

1

special meaning was "There Is Nothin' Like A Dame."

While the short bus ride into the city was fun, I failed to realize the full impact of that journey. The magic began the moment I entered the theater. Unlike some of the other students, all I could afford at the time was a seat in the back row of the highest balcony. As I climbed the steep stairs, settled into my seat and looked down to the stage so far below, I wondered how I could make sense of anything.

That worry disappeared when the house lights dimmed. A spotlight shown on the conductor in the orchestra pit and the audience applauded. This was all new to me, so I joined in with proper enthusiasm. The conductor bowed in appreciation, turned to the orchestra, waved his baton and the overture began.

From that moment, hearing the highlights of the well-known Rodgers and Hammerstein songs, I was transported to a mystical place that affected me through the years.

When the curtain rose, my "suspension of disbelief" took me to an island in the middle of the Pacific Ocean. World War II was raging and the actors became military personnel, nurses and South Sea Islanders dealing with their personal and actual war. My imagination transformed theater sets into real barracks, hospital rooms, the officers' club and island locations.

I must admit I was not prepared to appreciate the heart of the love story that dealt with racial prejudice and gave such power to the play. The full meaning of the song "You've Got To Be Carefully Taught," that portrays how bigotry passes from one generation to the next, escaped my awareness at the time.

I grew up in a section of Linden that was filled with immigrants from several European countries. My parents and brother and sister were born in what was then Czechoslovakia. My family migrated to Canada, where I was born, and then to the United States. All my playmates were first generation, hyphenated Americans: Hungarian-Americans, Italian-Americans, Irish-Americans, Scandinavian-Americans, among others. It would take many years before I came face-to-face with the ugliness of racial prejudice.

As the play unfolded, the music, characters, production numbers, costumes, settings, lightings and all the other theatrical trappings enveloped me in a way I had never experienced before. I was hooked.

After seeing *South Pacific* on the Broadway stage I discovered the allure of the theater would keep tugging at my thoughts and dreams.

The power of the show was so strong I went to college to study theater. After graduating, I pursued theater work in earnest and my resume included a variety of professional jobs in regional theaters and Off-Broadway.

Could a starring role on Broadway be far away?

As it turned out, that career dream was very far away.

So, was *South Pacific* a curse or blessing? Do I damn Rodgers and Hammerstein or thank them? Did my ambition for a theater career help or hinder me? Perhaps a little of both.

If I didn't take that high school drama department visit to Broadway, I may have been spared the agony of some painful catastrophes. But I would have missed the bliss of the pursuit which had its own rewards. It kept alive the idea that the dream might come true and inspired other dreams that did come true.

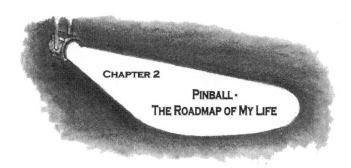

"Will you walk into my parlor,
said the Spider to the Fly;
'Tis the prettiest little parlor
that ever you did spy."
Mary Howitt

When I look back I think of how often I let chance
become my guiding force. Not unlike a pinball
bouncing off the rubber cushions and ricocheting
around the pinball machine. While bouncing around,
three significant events turned out to be very
fortunate for me. I wish I could say I had the insight
to plan them.

The first event occurred in my senior year of
high school. My good friend Tom asked me, "What
are your plans for college?"

"College?" I wondered. Oh, yeah, that might be a good idea. What should I do about it? Tom said, "You need to send in an application."

"Send an application," said I. "How do you do that?" Tom saw I was at a loss, so he helped me fill out the application to the college he attended, Rutgers University in New Brunswick, New Jersey. Then he made sure I mailed it.

My grades were good enough so I got admitted. At Rutgers I stumbled around as I adjusted to classes, campus life and even got accepted into Theta Chi fraternity. My fraternity brothers were an eclectic group of academics, jocks, party types, even some interested in theater. My close encounter with their varied backgrounds helped broaden my view of college experiences as well as give me some idea about life after college. We also had a few traditional frat socials, including a Roman style toga party.

I loved my French class and did well my first semester. How ironic I failed my first English class.

This had a sobering effect on me. I didn't have a problem with grammar or language. But I realized I just was not prepared for the analytical thought that my professor expected of me in my writing exercises. I retook the class in the summer and aced it. I must have learned something.

In my junior year my parents moved to Florida for health reasons, so I transferred to the

University of Miami in Coral Gables. Since I was required to take Reserve Officers' Training Corps (ROTC) at Rutgers, I continued the advanced training at Miami. This critical life-changing event happened quite by accident. During orientation week at Miami I passed tables set up for new students to get an idea of activities on campus. One of the tables was manned by ROTC cadets, so out of curiosity I stopped to chat.

Amazed I had already completed half of the requirements to receive a commission in the Army, a cadet said, "You'd be a fool not to sign up for the rest of the course." Not wanting to appear the fool, I signed up.

While joining the Army was the farthest idea in my head, I hoped I could get into the USO group that put on shows for our fighting soldiers. Someone had to do it. With my interest in theater and performing, why not me?

As an ROTC student I received an immediate benefit. The Army paid us a small allotment while we maintained our grades. Being strapped for cash became an ongoing ritual with me, so this seemed like a good short-term solution. I also got to use some surplus Army furniture which I needed for the off-campus apartment I rented.

With my ROTC courses completed, upon graduation, the Army sent me to Fort Benning,

Georgia for basic military training. It didn't take me long to learn the Army life was not for me.

Staying optimistic and having gone so far, I received a commission as a 2nd Lieutenant in the Ordnance Corps.

Next, the Army transferred me to Aberdeen Proving Ground in Maryland for officer's training. After the training I received there, the Army expected me to become an ordnance "expert" on weapons systems, ammunition, as well as procurement and maintenance of all wheeled and motored vehicles. With as much enthusiasm as I could muster up, I prepared to fulfil my two-year obligation of active duty.

The third event occurred when I finished this training. To find out where I would complete my active duty, I met with an assignment officer.

"Lieutenant Hrehovcik reporting as ordered," I gave the smartest salute I thought the moment deserved, which the captain returned as if brushing away a fly.

"Sit down, lieutenant, we're pretty informal here." The captain sat behind his report-laden desk as he waved me to the upright wooden chair opposite him. The office had a cramped, grey feel which seemed appropriate from all the war movies I had seen.

I settled into the chair eager to learn the location of my first assignment. This would be a major moment in the military career I had drifted into. I felt a little out of place. Not just here looking into the stern face of the captain. The whole idea of serving in the Army still seemed like a bit of a surprise. But I figured, if the United States Army believed I was ready to receive my first assignment, I'd go along with the idea.

The captain opened a folder that I scanned upside down. I saw my picture and several sheets of paper which must have documented my progress so far. He glanced at another folder. Reading upside down I managed to make out names of military posts around the world.

When other new officers from my unit came out of the captain's office, most had smiles and said they got plum assignments – Germany, England, even a few welcomed stateside locations like California and Florida.

I always wanted to visit Paris, so wouldn't it work out great if Uncle Sam sent me to deal with ordnance in some post in France. My imagination kicked into high gear. We weren't at war. It could be fun.

The captain looked up from my folder. I'm not sure, but I think he felt a little uneasy. "Would you mind if I sent you to South Korea?"

That's just how he said it. Like he asked my permission. This was new to me. The Army asking someone for permission. But that's the exact way he presented this new idea to me.

South Korea. I only had the vaguest clue where South Korea was located. Somewhere in the Far East on the other side of the world. Of course, I remembered the Korean War and all the misery it caused. But who thought of that now?

In a flash, a thousand ideas raced through my mind. So long Paris. So long Europe. So long cushy stateside posts. I made an effort to think of the upside. I'd probably never get a chance to go to the Far East on my own. Maybe it could be an adventure. My thoughts came to a stop. The captain waited.

South Korea. Why not? I made a decision. "Sure." I managed a smile.

The captain looked surprised and a bit relieved. I think he had a quota to fill and this might be the toughest one on his list.

So, off I went to South Korea. There remained a Demarcation Military Zone at the 38th Parallel we had to protect. It divided South Korea from North Korea. It's still there.

Lucky for me we weren't at war at the time. I'm sure I would have been shot. No doubt by my own troops. The Army expects you to do more than show up. You have to be a soldier. This may have been my best acting performance.

I got a good indication Army life did not fit into my future during a Christmas party in the officers' club near the end of my tour in South Korea in 1962. Food and drinks created a relaxed atmosphere. I listened as officers shared "war stories" of their assignments around the world. Pretty soon the group broke into an energetic version of the "Caisson's Song," the Army's theme song. It was then, as they got into the spirit of the song I realized how much these officers loved what they were doing. I could tell from the intensity of their singing, they felt a great pride in the important job they carried out and the honorable tradition they revered. Their singing came from their deepest, personal feelings, from their hearts.

I felt sad and a little envious that I could not become a part of their world. My heart belonged in a different place. I knew deep down I could never share their love of the Army. I knew I didn't belong. All I could do was do my best until my discharge date. When it came I could not have been happier. Yet, I also knew I left behind a group of men I admired and felt honored to have them as a part of my life.

When my two years of active duty ended and a recruitment officer asked me if I wanted to pursue a military career, it took only a split second to say, "No, sir."

13

An excellent decision for both me and the Army.

I wish I could say I made the decisions to go to college, sign up for the ROTC course and take a military assignment in South Korea were a result of conscious goal setting and realistic future planning. Instead, it had all the folly and senselessness of a spinning pinball in its aimless trek hoping to rack up some points. Pinball became a metaphor of my life. All too often I'd get mesmerized by the flashing lights and distracted by the deafening sound effects. Sometimes I'd get a decent score, but all too often the game ended up: "TILT."

"... the dream is the theater where the dreamer is at once scene, actor, prompter, stage manager, author, audience, and critic.
Carl Jung

The span of the Hudson River between New Jersey and New York City measures about a mile and a half. One short distance for a man, one giant chasm for the clueless faint of heart.

I grew up in New Jersey with dreams of becoming an actor. My older brother Mike asked me, "Why don't you just cross the river and audition for a part in a play on Broadway?" My brother had lots of helpful advice. He could be very annoying.

With a degree in theater arts from the University of Miami and a couple of theater jobs on my resume, you'd think a visit to Broadway would seem like a logical approach to fulfill my dream.

15

But crossing the Hudson River in the 1960s to find an acting job never occurred to me. Perhaps, deep in my heart I never thought I had the talent to compete with the likes of Dick Van Dyke, Robert Preston, Richard Burton and other experienced actors performing at the time.

So instead, after I got out of the Army in 1962, I traveled to Chicago to audition for a series of regional theaters that held joint tryouts once a year. It gave actors an opportunity to present their talents to at least twenty different theaters from across the country.

The odds seemed good. No doubt at least one theater company producer would recognize my comic and dramatic skills.

I felt lucky that two did. With hopes high, I drove the 530 miles from Chicago to Memphis, Tennessee to the theater that seemed most promising. On the way to Memphis I crossed the Mississippi River, just to say I did it.

During the interview the producer asked, "So, Steve, what's your area of expertise?"

Eager to impress him, I said, "I just love the theater. I can do anything you need."

This turned out to be the wrong answer. He wanted specialists, like a sound designer, lighting technician or stage manager. My enthusiasm didn't impress him.

So back to Chicago I trekked. I visited another theater that showed interest at my audition. There I met with the same unhappy result. I started to get the clue that theater would be a rough mistress.

Devastated, I continued to make the rounds of theaters in the area. After a lot of searching I found a small theater northeast of Chicago, in Arlington Heights. A millionaire who made his fortune with a drug store chain had a passion for the theater. He converted the back room of a bowling alley into an intimate three-quarter stage theater. That's where the stage is positioned against one wall and the audience surrounds three sides.

It had about fifty seats, with no offstage or area for scenery. He expected the audience to use its imagination a lot. Not the theater image I envisioned, but he needed a stage manager. Ben, his current stage manager, decided to move on, giving short notice.

While it wasn't acting, it was the THEATER. This time my interview may have been one of my best performances. The producer asked, "Have you ever stage-managed before?"

"Sure," I said, and rattled off several backstage technical terms I learned over the years, like, "spotlight gels," "proscenium arch," and "green room."

Either I convinced him I could do the job or he was desperate. Either way, to my great delight he hired me.

At last I had arrived in a professional company and got paid – not much – but enough to rent a room in a private home and eat on a regular schedule.

The theater company consisted of a small group of talented actors and me. Not only did I serve as stage manager, I found props, recorded sound, designed sets and lighting and got coffee during breaks. I loved it – at first.

But something didn't seem right. I yearned for more. So I quit, even though I had no other job pending.

How many times had I heard my brother Mike tell me: "Never quit a job unless you have a better one waiting for you." Great advice, which I seldom heeded. I got good at quitting promising jobs without a clue of what would happen next.

Once again I went auditioning at other theaters around Chicago. When no one recognized my brilliance and money got short, I decided I needed some kind of job – any job. I broadened my search and visited an employment agency. The interviewer asked me, "Can you write? Spiegel Catalog needs a copywriter."

Recalling college term papers and student plays I'd written, I said, "Write, sure I can write." Another great performance.

Maybe he needed to fill his allotment for the month, so he arranged an interview. When I arrived at Spiegel I took a test to create an ad for a child's toy. Some instinct told me to write the word "Fun" in the headline. It seemed like a logical way to describe a way to play with this child's toy.

To this day I believe that my use of that magic word - "Fun" – got me the copywriting job. While elated, I admit I was a bit surprised. At the time I had no clue I had a latent talent to write advertising copy.

I don't remember dressing with any particular flair, what with my limited financial resources, but for reasons known only to Spiegel's inner circle, they placed me in the men's fashion department. How hard could it be? You want cuffs on these pants?

It seemed to work. To describe men's clothing I discovered two adjectives – "smart" and "handsome" - that I slipped into my copy whenever no one was looking. I'd write: Wear this smart jacket. You'll look handsome. Or: Wear this handsome jacket. You'll look smart. Or: Wear this jacket. You'll look smart and handsome.

Spiegel had a lot to offer as a place to work. But, restless again and itching to get back into the theater, I quit right after they offered me a raise.

Ignoring my brother Mike's advice was getting to be a habit.

I decided if I couldn't find a job in professional theater, I'd go back to school. Maybe I'd find a teaching job in a college theater department.

Somewhere I heard that Catholic University in Washington, D.C. had a top-notch theater department. I applied and got accepted. Perhaps my years as an altar boy hanging around the holy water helped.

I didn't have any money for tuition, but my career as a professional stage manager – even for six months - got me a working scholarship. My lack of funds also qualified me for a student loan. At the time this came as a godsend. But like so many graduates discovered, the loan became a brutal drain to repay afterward.

Not only did I meet the challenge of a strict collegiate discipline, I met a remarkable lady, Carol Dispenza. We shared a number of classes. Like me, she loved the theater, but had a much more practical view of her prospects. Carol's goal from the start was to teach theater at a private school or college. She already had a teacher's certificate from her undergraduate studies and already taught in several schools including dependents of Army soldiers in Germany.

We started out with a workable arrangement. She had books, which I couldn't afford, and I had a car. I borrowed her books and she let me chauffeur her and me to classes and back.

One thing led to another, then another, and before you knew it love blossomed. Soon after that we decided to elope. We drove ninety miles from Washington, D.C. to Elkton, Maryland and got married. We could have just crossed the border into Silver Spring, Maryland, but Elkton, made famous for elopements, seemed more romantic.

Both our families reacted in shock and anger. It took a while for Carol's family to accept me, sort of. My traditional parents took longer to get used to me married to Carol. I heard some gossip that said, "It'll be over in two years."

With a wife and soon the birth of a new baby, our son Joshua, to support, it started to sink in that the theater may not hold the best prospects to bring up a family.

Ever eager to point out the error of my ways, my brother Mike, back in New Jersey, again offered advice: "Come back to Jersey, I can help you get a decent job."

For once I took his advice, because with it came that magic word – a job. Mike had a career as a plastic products designer and was about to start on a new project. He needed support designers to fill out his team. Mike knew I had some design abilities. I got them by osmosis working construction with my father. It took another great performance to demonstrate I knew how to handle a T-square and triangle.

The job offered a decent pay and seemed like a promising career move, unless, of course, you had a silly notion that your destiny depended on the theater. The job was located in the Bronx. The fact that the Bronx is not far from Broadway did not escape my attention. Our work commute took us across that chasm-wide Hudson River. How ironic.

We found a rental in Lodi, then Rutherford, New Jersey. Except for attending a few shows on Broadway, I stifled my lust for the theater while the design job continued.

A short time later, while walking in New York City's theater district, I bumped into Ben, the guy I had replaced as a stage manager back in the Arlington Heights bowling alley theater. What luck I thought. Although, when I told Carol, she didn't think it so lucky.

Ben had come to New York seeking his fortune in the theater and told me about an Off-Broadway show that served as a showcase for promising talent. They needed crew members and actors for a small part.

My heart skipped a beat. Could this be my entrance to the big-time? Could this be some cosmic force at work? Could I be nuts to even consider such a long shot?

Even though the project leader of the plastic company offered me a permanent position as a designer, guess what I did? I thanked the project leader and told him I had to jump at this unexpected opportunity.

Carol did not share my excitement. Especially when I told her the job offered no pay, just potential. Carol said something to the effect, "Are you crazy?" I refused to see her skepticism and barreled ahead. Needless to say, in the tradition of theater lore, the lead of the show did not break his foot on opening night, requiring me to take his place and save the show. When the curtain came down at the end of the short run, it also came down on my brief Off-Broadway career.

This zigzag pattern between good-paying jobs and non-paying theater prospects repeated itself an embarrassing number of times. You'd think after a few disappointments and disasters I'd get a clue.

How Carol put up with all these calamities is still a mystery to me. To be fair, somehow I must have managed enough encouraging moments along the way – along with two more children, our son Noah and daughter Gillian. It seems appropriate to describe my *modus operandi* in theatrical terms. In 1971, a revival of the musical "No, No, Nanette" became an instant hit. Borrowing from that show's title to describe the gambles I ventured, you could say I took dangerous risks like walking a tightrope with "No, No, Net!"

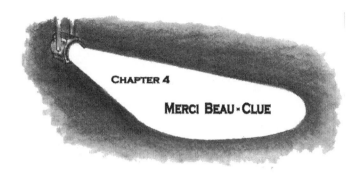

"A fool must now and then be right, by chance."
William Cowper

The mystery of my dyslexia patterns evaded my attention until I discovered I words mixed up. I got a clue when rehearsing a play. I'd come across dialogue that might say, "Let's go to the house." Instead I would say, "Let's go home." It's sort of the same thing, but authors get incensed when you mangle their precious words. It didn't make the actors I appeared with happy either.

This word substitution caused endless problems when the word "house" served as the cue for the next actor's line. I didn't realize anything was amiss until a fellow actor alerted me to my predicament.

After we finished our scene together when we headed backstage, he said, "If you don't say the right lines I'm going to punch you in the nose."

By the intensity of his words, the glare in his eyes and clenched fist, I knew he wasn't acting.

Such mix-ups happened so often I got suspicious and began to wonder if there lurked a deeper meaning to my dyslexia than just confused words. Did I suffer from a dyslexia of life?

Perhaps when I thought I saw a marvelous opportunity, was it in fact a marred lunacy? It would take many foolish blunders before I got the clue.

In 1968 I quit another good job where I worked as advertising manager for a company in New York City that dealt with the hobby of stamp collecting.

By this time, we had our second son Noah. Carol and I had become discontented with living in New Jersey and my making the daily commute to the city. Theater options dried up and our landlord just sold the house we rented. We had a month to vacate. With nothing more than a strong desire for a change, we moved into the top floor of the three-story apartment building Carol's parents owned in Bradford, Massachusetts. I figured I'd find a job someplace.

My New Jersey family just about gave up on me. But I had gotten used to that.

With my steady ad manager's job, we managed to save a few dollars, but it was drying up fast. While the Boston theater scene tempted me, by now I knew I needed a more substantial "civilian" job.

My ability to improvise gave me an advantage to meet people and network with ease. At one social gathering I flitted around eavesdropping on conversations, listening for clues from someone who might have a job opportunity.

I overheard a man say he had connections in the advertising world. I introduced myself and told him about my experiences in advertising.

I guess I impressed him enough because he said, "They're looking for an ad manager at a bank in Cambridge. I'll arrange an interview for you."

With the man's introduction I met the bank's human resources manager. After a few tests and more interviews, I got the bank job as advertising manager. My dyslexia might have presented a problem if I worked as a bank teller. Imagine a customer making a deposit of "$1,573,223" and I marked it up as "$15,732.23."

The job had some advantages - a steady paycheck and a few perks, like employee discounts on auto loans.

I'm not sure why I got hired. Almost from the start my boss and I never quite hit it off. He had a domineering personality that I never could figure out. After a while it became obvious that the officers of the bank were in the middle of a power struggle. Clueless me, I got caught in the middle of the fireworks.

A short time after I started, one of the many senior vice presidents asked me to write a press release about a new service the bank offered. So I wrote it. Unbeknownst to me, this new service did not fit into the vision my immediate boss had for the new direction he intended to take the bank. So when he got wind of my press release he called me on the carpet and it seemed ready to sweep me under it.

From that point on I could never fathom what he wanted of me, because he gave me silly jobs like organizing files. I did some work with the bank's advertising agency, but it entailed carrying messages back and forth to the boss. He humored me by allowing me to interview salespeople who had services they wanted to sell to the bank. Of course, I had no authority to buy anything, just get the details so the salesmen wouldn't fritter away my boss's time.

One day an advertising salesman came by selling space in a local magazine. After we chatted a bit, I learned we were kindred spirits. When not selling, he acted in a local community theater.

Soon our conversation switched from advertising to what's new in the area's theater world. I sat on the edge of my chair when he mentioned he knew someone who planned to start a new theater in Maine. A new theater meant new staff, actors and crews.

Since the bank had lost its allure as a career move, perhaps I could check out the possibilities with the new theater people. The salesman gave me the name of the producer, a woman. To my delight, she lived a short distance from the bank.

I arranged an interview and gave one of my convincing performances again. While I had hoped to become the director of the new company, she already had that position filled. But she needed someone to help raise funds and coordinate publicity.

Perfect. I could do that. I could do anything in THE THEATER.

I did it again. I quit my decent paying job at the bank to chase that theater rainbow. Carol didn't share my enthusiasm. But she knew there would be no stopping me to follow this dream. So, instead of the hour-plus commute from our home in Bradford to the bank in Cambridge, I swapped it for an hour-and-a-half commute to Portland, Maine. For a lot less money.

But, after a month, I made a grievous error by challenging the producer on how she was running the theater. So she fired me. Driving home on the Maine Turnpike I dreaded the idea of telling Carol. I let her down, again.

My thoughts were a muddle as I approached the turnpike exit at Kennebunkport. I heard some theater buzz that new producers had just bought the former Kennebunkport Playhouse. While the playhouse had been dark for a few years, it once featured major stars in plays during the summer months.

I had been driving in the passing lane as I approached the exit. Thinking fast, at the last minute I swerved into the exit ramp just missing a few cars. I found the playhouse with a phone number on the sign of the real estate agency that sold the playhouse. After a few phone calls I arranged for an interview with the two new owners, who happened to live a few towns away from our apartment in Bradford.

Performance time again. I got the job as the theater's advertising and public relations manager. I moved the family into a shoebox cottage for the summer on Goose Rocks Beach, a wide sandy ocean-front section of Kennebunkport. I didn't know it then, but tourists had been coming to this area for their summer vacations. Carol and the boys had a chance to enjoy the long scenic beach.

The new theater owners had years of experience in community theater, but were more naïve than me about running the playhouse. It didn't help that the serious dramas they selected didn't fit into the traditional lighthearted themes audiences expected. The season was a disaster and closed a week prior to its advertised schedule.

As part of my promotion work for the theater I got on good terms with the advertising manager of the York County Coast Star, the weekly paper of the area. He had decided to return to teaching and the paper was looking for someone to replace him. They offered me the job.

In spite of the headaches, uncertainties and mix-ups of the summer, Carol and I found we had come to like the area. "Why don't we stay and make our home here?" I asked Carol.

It didn't take long for her to say, "Yes, this could be a good place to live."

So, in 1970 I found a three-bedroom house to rent. It had a large yard, split rail fence and was a short distance from the beach. This was the first house Carol ever lived in. We loved it.

Perhaps my dyslexic lifestyle could work to our benefit. The area, popular with summer vacationers, had a renowned shipbuilding tradition and streets lined with classic historic buildings. One massive structure had been converted into a funeral home. Little could I know of more mix-ups just around the coroner.

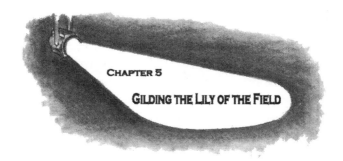

"It takes little talent to see clearly what lies under one's nose ..."
Wystan Hugh Auden

"Showing up is 80 percent ..."
Attributed to *Woody Allen*

For some reason I misinterpreted Woody Allen's observation about "Showing up is 80 percent." I added a twist. I don't know why, but I figured all I had to do was show up and people would love me. Perhaps "love me" comes off a little strong. But I took it as some sort of given that since I had the good sense to show up, people would recognize my brilliance and defer to my whims and wishes.

Of course, this made no sense at all on a rational level. Even after some embarrassing

33

meetings, it took some time to get the clue that I had to earn my way with a good performance. I refer not only to a theatrical performance.

I know I never had this expectation of divine benevolence on a conscious level. It seemed rather some sort of feeling like I had an entitlement based on my youthful exposure to a biblical passage I heard in a sermon in church. It comes from the gospel of Matthew 6:28. "Consider the lilies of the field, how they grow; they toil not, neither do they spin. Even Solomon in all his glory was not arrayed like one of these."

Just imagine how this powerful image can influence a developing mind. After all, should I doubt Matthew in all his authority?

It's obvious I let the lilies passage trump Matthew's other description of the parable Jesus told about the man who gave talents to his slaves to invest. When I first heard this story I didn't realize "talent" was a term for money, compounding my confusion. The slaves who invested wisely, he rewarded. One slave hid his talent in a hole for safety. The man punished this slave for his timidity.

The story of the lilies in the field affected my impressionable mind with unimaginable power. The lesson of a generous God taking care of all my needs reached me on some deep, unexplainable level. Yet, as with so many others of life's lessons, I missed the point. I took them literally, too literally. And this caused me years of grief, even though the clues of this lesson were all around me. I simply preferred not to heed them.

Perhaps it would be more appropriate to say the parable of the lilies impaired me. In fact, they ruined a great deal of my ambition during my growing years. I interpreted them to mean that I didn't need to really do anything. All I had to do was show up. Everything else would be taken care of. I had the Gospel's word on it.

But the words also caused me a great deal of confusion. For I learned from watching my father and mother struggle to provide for my brother and sister and me that life required a *lot* of hard work. You can imagine my dilemma. On the one hand God says you do not have to toil or spin. But at the same time my father worked two jobs and my mother worked as a seamstress.

I didn't want to doubt the word of God. This would mean burning in Hell. I really believed in Hell, even as my father worked like hell to feed and clothe our family. The real problem from the paradox I faced arose because I believed, truly believed both messages. One message told me, don't worry. The other, worry.

This dual message may have been the seed of the doubts and indecisions that plagued a great deal of my life. It caused me to change careers on a whim, move about the country chasing rainbows and sliding from one debacle to another.

Digging deeper into my psyche, my lily's image came in direct conflict with the belief that I wasn't "good enough." So when I did not achieve the expectations I had for "showing up," it caused no lack of confusion and bewilderment.

One of the disastrous results of my belief in Woody Allen's quotation "Showing up is 80 percent ..." gave me the impression that I didn't need to prepare with any degree of effort. When I arrived at several auditions I figured I could wing it and I'd dazzle 'em. Well, dazzled they weren't.

What I was, was puzzled.

How come they couldn't see beyond the surface to see the depth of my inner talent? It took the embarrassment of several dreadful auditions, as well as other non-theater job searches where my lack of preparation led to bitter disappointment.

Once I interviewed at an advertising agency for a designer position. The manager gave me a test to see how I used colors to create an image. He handed me a drawing of a living room with the furniture, windows, wall pictures and other features outlined in pen, not unlike a child's coloring book. He also gave me a number of colored pens. All I had to do was fill in harmonizing colors between the lines. How hard could that be?

Well, I froze and couldn't figure out where to start. I feared I'd make a mistake, so I did nothing. A half hour later the manager came to check on my progress. I had nothing to show him. I didn't add a single color to the page.

I slinked out of the office, embarrassed and ashamed. I started to get a clue that I needed to prepare a little better for my next interview.

LILY! COME BACK AND LOOK BEAUTIFUL. OUT THERE THEY SPIN AND TOIL!

CHAPTER 6

WHERE DID THE GIRLS GO?

"Something hidden. Go and find it.
Go and look behind the Ranges –
Something lost behind the Ranges.
Lost and waiting for you. Go!"
Rudyard Kipling

When looking for clues, it can be very frustrating. They can lie hidden in the strangest places. It's just a matter of knowing two things. First: realize that there's a clue out there, somewhere, that can help you solve a problem. Second: find it.

It reminds me of the story I heard about two boy ostriches. They happen to see two girl ostriches in a clearing a short distance away.

One boy ostrich says to the other boy ostrich, "Hey, look. Two girl ostriches. Let's go meet them." So the two boy ostriches start a casual stroll toward the two girl ostriches.

One of the girl ostriches sees the boys approaching and says to the other girl ostrich, "Look. There are two boy ostriches heading our way. Let's hide." So the two girl ostriches bury their heads in the sand.

The two boy ostriches come up behind the two girl ostriches. One of the boy ostriches searches around with a puzzled look on his face. He turns to the other boy ostrich and says, "Where did the girls go?"

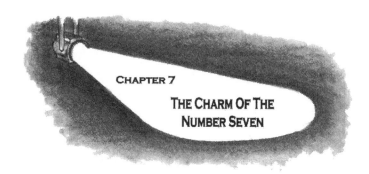

"Seven is a good, handy figure in its way,
picturesque, with a savor of the mythical ..."
The Magic Mountain, Thomas Mann

"If you keep a thing seven years,
you are sure to find a use for it."
Woodstock, Sir Walter Scott

I only got a clue a short time ago how the number seven had a curious recurring significance in my life. At age seven I sat at our kitchen table in Linden, New Jersey, to draw my first picture. I had scribbled fun shapes as part of learning how to use a pencil and practice writing plenty of times. I didn't realize it at the time, but this picture at the kitchen table became the start of my art career which continues to this day.

The picture took the shape of a convertible jalopy. I copied it from a drawing made by a friend of

41

my brother Mike. I drew the wheels first, then the bent fenders and ragged torn top. When I got the general shape done I added steam rising from the radiator cap and puffs of smoke erupting from the exhaust pipe. These touches were my own idea. I felt so proud. To me it looked like a masterpiece.

My brother seemed impressed with my drawing and encouraged me to keep at it. I would redraw that jalopy many times. Sometimes I'd color it with crayons. Other times I'd just redraw it, faster each time.

About the same time, I began watching a television show called *You Are An Artist*. On our 12" black and white set I sat mesmerized as I followed artist Jon Gnagy give step-by-step instructions on how to draw simple pictures – a dog, a clown, a river scene. Most often, from the first outline to the finished drawing it took seven steps. In one of my favorite shows Gnagy taught me how to draw a covered bridge. The picture of the bridge stretching across a stream would be my introduction to perspective, a technique I still use today when I draw homes and buildings.

The significance of the number seven reoccurred when I started the seventh grade. Most of our classes were co-ed. But, for one class, the boys and girls went to separate rooms in different parts of the school. The boys would build model planes and the girls would draw pictures. I had no problem with planes, but after the first class I lost interest. My real desire was to get into the art class.

I should add that my self-esteem needed a lot of encouragement at the time. So you can imagine the nerve it took for me to ask my teacher if I could switch to the art class. I feared she would feel insulted that I didn't like her or her class. To my surprise, she agreed and told me to join the art students.

The art class was on the third floor about 100 miles away. I recall the long walk to the door of the classroom. Hands sweating, I turned the knob and opened the door. I took a step into the room and all the girls looked up from their work. I imagined they were taken a bit back to see a boy infringe on their girly domain. With all the determination I could muster, I walked to the art teacher, introduced myself and said I had permission to join the art class. She smiled and told me to take a seat and start drawing something.

I settled into one of the back chairs, feeling a little awkward as the only boy in the class. Then a surprise happened. The door opened and three more boys entered. They preferred to take the art class instead of building planes, too. I guess I became something of a pathfinder. I always felt a certain pride when the teacher mentioned there was no need for art to be restricted to the girls.

Of course, in addition to learning about art, I didn't mind being surrounded by a bunch of girls.

There were more than seven of them and sometimes it would be difficult to concentrate on the subject I was drawing. But it added to the fun.

By sheer coincidence the number seven came into play again, although several years later. When I was 17 I walked past an abandoned car by the side of the road near my home. Perhaps because it was a convertible and reminded me of the jalopy I had drawn so many years ago, I fell in love with it.

I had my driver's license and drove my father's car, a 1957 Chevy, when he didn't use it. But what a thrill it would be to have my own set of wheels. I found out who owned the car and asked if he'd sell it. He told me it hadn't been driven in years. It would take a lot of work to get it drivable.

My brother Mike came to my rescue. He had an entrepreneurial nature and became the manager of a gas station. I had saved a few dollars, but, thanks to my father, who recognized my enthusiasm for the car, helped me finance it. The owner wanted $100 for it. But since it was in such bad shape my father bargained him down to $70. I think the owner was just glad to be rid of it.

We hauled the car to my brother's station and together we rebuilt it. I had no idea what I was doing. I just followed my brother's directions. It took a while of dedicated work. At last we got it running, cleaned up the inside and painted it a bright red. It became my commuter car when I started to commute to the

Rutgers campus in New Brunswick in 1957. And the car – a Ford, 1947.

Jumping ahead with sevens, we moved to Maine in 1970, so in 2017 we'll have lived here for 47 years.

One more series of sevens. As I write these memories I've reached the age of 77.

I'm thinking of getting a lottery ticket with a bunch of sevens.

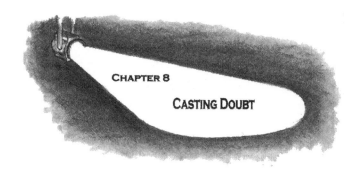

"Oh would some Power the giftie give us
To see ourselves as others see us."
From *"To A Louse"* by *Robert Burns*

One of my first acting auditions came when our church planned to perform *The Passion of The Christ*. Our new priest had a reputation for staging *The Passion* at other parishes, so it came as no surprise when he announced the search for actors and crews from the pulpit.

As an acting student I figured I had an edge over the others for the top role of Jesus. After all, didn't I just complete a semester of college as a drama major? My competitors were mere parishioners.

It came as quite a shock that the parish priest, who would be directing the pageant, had typecast me to play the part of Judas. How humiliating. This was a blow to my spiritual ego. How could the priest not see me portraying the Son of God? Perhaps I may not have had the appearance of Jesus. But does anyone really know what He looked like? I figured with a little makeup, beard, robe and a few trick props, I could change water into wine with the best of them.

At the time I did not realize what a plum role like Judas could do for my career. This is long before I learned that most accolades and Oscars went to deviates, prostitutes and some of civilizations more destructive personalities. Nevertheless, I felt crushed.

This experience, however, did set the stage for me to realize that the image I had of myself did not match what others saw in me. Was there something I was missing in my opinion of myself?

As a drama student at the University of Miami I played several character roles. A murderer in *Macbeth*, three different roles in *As You Like It* and a grumpy butler in *Major Barbara*. I even won the Best Actor Award for my portrayal of the lead in the farce *Hotel Paradiso*.

In need of some reassurance I asked my professor if he thought I had what it takes to make it in the theater. He said, "Look in the mirror and see what type you think you are."

I looked in the mirror and saw Cary Grant looking back. So, I went for leading roles. Talk about delusion. I realize now I should have looked for character roles played by actors like Jimmy Durante,

Huntz Hall of the Bowery Boys fame, John Belushi or Dustin Hoffman. Or bad guys like the early Richard Widmark or Christopher Lee.

The only saving grace occurred when our priest cancelled *The Passion* play because of a lack of participants. I was spared my embarrassment in portraying Judas, which, for all I know, could have been my breakout performance. I think I rationalized since I didn't get to play the part of Jesus this time, maybe there would be a more appropriate role down the road.

It just goes to show you. The acting gods work in mysterious ways.

"Thus conscience doth make cowards of us all ..."
William Shakespeare

"Ofttimes nothing profits more than self-esteem,
grounded on just and right well manag'd."
John Milton

Self-esteem never occurred to me. I didn't have a
clue that I was supposed to have any. In fact, I had a
lot of trouble believing I had any self-worth at all. Just
the opposite. The signs of my negative image began
to show up in my early teenage years.

I recall when I graduated from junior high
school I went to the local Woolworth's 5 & 10
department store to buy school supplies so I'd be
ready for high school. It felt exciting to start classes
and I wanted to be prepared for the unknown waiting
for me.

As I roamed the store aisles looking over the selections of pencils, pens and pads I came to the item that would stop me cold in my tracks – binders. Woolworth's offered a variety of covers and styles. I examined them all and noticed that some binders had posts for two-hole paper and others had posts for three-hole paper.

Which do I pick? Two-post or three-post. It held me spellbound for quite some time. Both styles of binders cost the same, so that didn't concern me. So did the paper. Two-hole paper costs the same as the three-hole paper. What a dilemma.

After considerable mental anguish I made my decision. I picked the two-post binder and two-hole paper. I figured the two-hole paper was good enough for me. I didn't deserve the three-hole paper. How pathetic.

To think I had so little sense of my self-worth that I settled for two-hole paper instead of three-hole. If something so irrelevant as the difference between two-hole and three-hole paper could hold such an influence on me, can you imagine what would happen when I would face a serious problem?

Such a problem did occur a short time later. Since I would soon enter the halls of my high school I felt I would need to act like an adult. I needed a wallet.

At that same Woolworth's department store I went to the section where they displayed wallets. I didn't have a problem finding a wallet I liked. But when I opened the wallet to examine the sections for holding money and cards I noticed a card that had a printed section where I'd put my name and address. No problem so far..

But just below that section, the card had a space where I would put the name of a person to call in case of an emergency. What to do? I couldn't think of anyone's name I should put down. I thought the logical person I should list would be my father. But after considering it for a while, I decided I didn't want to bother him.

Can you imagine the depth of my loneliness? Not wanting to bother my father in case I had an emergency. After an agonizing time, I decided to put the name of my sister Anne in that section. If necessary, she'd tell my father. Fortune must have smiled on me, because I never had to use that "in case of emergency" section in my wallet. What a relief I didn't have to bother my father.

There's another time I dismissed my value as a person. I loved to sing and I guess I had a pretty good voice. I sang in the church choir and high school choral groups. I even got selected for the New Jersey All-State Chorus, which was a pretty big deal for me.

With my love of music and apparent ability, during my freshman year at Rutgers University, I figured I could get into the men's chorus. Then I learned that each singer had to buy his own red jacket. There was no way I could afford a jacket or ask my father for money to buy one. So for want of a jacket I decided not to audition for the chorus.

What a pity.

I could not tell how many opportunities I let slip by because of my poor self-image. Even more amazing to me is that I managed to accomplish anything at all. The inner struggle never stopped.

Perhaps part of my natural maturing helped me overcome some of this timidity. Perhaps that's the reason I became drawn to the theater. I had to pretend to be a different character when I acted. There's no way of knowing for sure, but there's a possibility I got drawn to the theater to salvage my life from an overblown image of poverty, scarcity and self-denial.

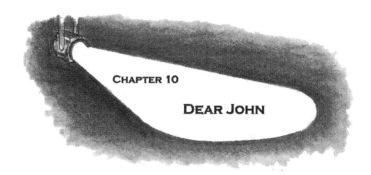

"Be not the first by whom the new are tried,
Nor the last to lay the old aside."
Alexander Pope

"I am amaz'd, methinks, and lose my way
Among the thorns and danger of this world."
William Shakespeare

Imagine my surprise on the first day of class at
Linden Junior High School. Eager, but somewhat
uncertain about leaving my small elementary school
behind, I entered my seventh grade home room and
sat at an unoccupied desk. I introduced myself to the
boy next to me, "Hi, I'm Steve."

He said, "Hi, I'm George." We made some
idle conversation waiting for our lady teacher to take
attendance. After she got us settled down, she read
names from her list. I noticed the pattern of names

coming in alphabetical order, by last names. She got to the letter "H" so I got ready to say, "Here." I expected her to hesitate when she got to "Hrehovcik" since it's a difficult name to pronounce the first time you see it. I'd gotten used to this.

She called out, "John," and hesitated as she tried to pronounce the last name. I wondered who had a difficult name like mine. The teacher apologized because she didn't want to say the name wrong so she started to spell it. "H-R-E-H-O ..."

I smiled as I recognized the first few letters of my last name and called out, "Hrehovcik. It's pronounced 'Hero – check.' But who is John?"

She looked at me with a puzzled expression and asked, "Are you John Hrehovcik?"

I said, "No, I'm Steve Hrehovcik."

She glanced down at the attendance sheet again and a smile of recognition came across her face. "Oh, I see," she said, "You are John Stephen Hrehovcik. Steve is your middle name."

"Middle name?" My obvious confusion caused laughter to ripple through the room. "No," I insisted, "Steve is my first name. I don't have a middle name."

"It's down here on the attendance sheet as 'John Stephen Hrehovcik.' We'll sort it out later." She gave a reassuring smile and went on to take attendance of the rest of the class.

And that's how I learned my first name is John. Never in all my thirteen years on this earth did I have an inkling I had a first name of John. How could this happen? I figured out later that our family had so many men named "John," my parents called me by my middle name to avoid confusion.

After I got over the embarrassment of that dubious start of my seventh grade, I decided to embrace the name "John." This could be fun. Kind of like discovering a whole new person. When I met a new classmate I introduced myself as "John." This turned out to have some confusing results. When I bumped into former classmates and friends from my elementary school who knew me as "Steve" it took some explaining about my real first name and how I just discovered it.

It got trickier because some students knew me as John, others knew me as Steve. Then someone hearing both names came up with the idea to call me "JohnSteve," like it was one word. Not to be outdone, others from my original group came up with "SteveJohn." Each name became a nickname. What started out as embarrassing and confusing gave me a minor celebrity status. I admit I enjoyed the attention.

While this entire experience with name confusion had its bright side, at some quiet moments I wondered, "How come no one ever mentioned I had the name John? And why did I have to learn about it in such an undignified way?"

It bothered me even more that I didn't have the nerve to ask my family about it. My low self-esteem had gotten me into a pattern of believing that's the way it was supposed to be. I accepted this blissful ignorance as normal. And since I had the fun of my friends christening me with my new nicknames, I pushed the importance of not knowing into the background.

Today, I still introduce myself as "Steve," although for official matters, like signing checks, driver's license and legal documents, I sign "John S. Hrehovcik." This creates new problems with modern phone identities. When I call someone, they see the name "John S. Hrehovcik" on their phone display and they ask the same question I asked back in junior high school, "Who is John?" I explain it's their old buddy "Steve" and we can get on with the conversation.

Years later I experienced a similar identity problem with more sinister consequences. During the summer between my junior and senior years at the University of Miami, I lived with my parents in Lake Worth, Florida, just south of Palm Beach. Desperate for work, I got a temporary job with a company that sold window awnings for residential homes. My job required me and my co-workers to knock on doors and hand out pamphlets describing the marvelous features, advantages and benefits of shading windows from the blistering hot Florida sun.

It seemed easy enough. My co-workers and I fanned out in our assigned neighborhood. As I walked through my area I looked for houses with exposed windows. I figured the sweating residents of these homes made the ideal candidates. I knocked on the door and hoped for a welcoming smile. It seemed to be going well. I gave out quite a few brochures. One considerate elderly lady even invited me in for a drink of cold water. I accepted and after a relaxing drink and small conversation I left the house. To my surprise, at the curb I saw a police car. Crammed into the back seat sat my co-workers. "What's going on?" I thought. Later I learned the section of town we chose to hand out pamphlets had a regulation against home solicitation.

The policeman motioned for me to get into the car. I got in and we took a short ride to the police station. It all seemed unreal. At the station, one of the detectives asked me questions, like I've seen in so many cops and robbers movies, except a bit more relaxed. At first I was amused. After all, what had I done wrong? Must be some kind of mistake. Then he asked me the question that changed everything. He asked me where I was born.

I said, "Canada."

He hesitated a bit, then asked, "Where's your Green Card?"

I asked, "What's a Green Card?"

He said, "You don't have a Green Card?"

Puzzled, I shook my head "No."

He turned to another detective at the next desk with a concerned look and said to him, "Looks like we have a wetback here."

I had no idea what he was talking about. He looked at me and said, "If you're an immigrant and you work in America on a permanent basis you have to have a Green Card. Since you don't have the card, you may be a guest of the United States government by spending the night in jail."

"Jail!" I blurted. "What do you mean spend the night in jail? What did I do wrong? I was just working a summer job."

He asked me a few more personal questions, wrote some notes on his pad, all the while exchanging grim glances with the other detective. I didn't know whether to laugh or panic. After a few more questions and a long agonizing pause, the detective at the next desk shrugged and said, "Let him go." I guess he realized I was not a threat to our national security.

I couldn't leave fast enough. Outside the police station the owner of the awning company sat in his car with the rest of my co-workers. He drove us back to the company. On the ride back the others had a big laugh at the entire episode. Not me. I realized how out of touch I was. How come I didn't know about Green Cards and how being born in Canada made me a "wetback?"

I didn't mention any of this to my parents when I got home. I felt too embarrassed to tell them I almost landed in jail. At first I became angry at them, as well as my brother and sister. They were all born in Czechoslovakia. They must have needed Green Cards for work. Why wouldn't they tell me about it? Or when I applied for jobs I must have included where I was born on the application. Why wouldn't the employers ask me about my Green Card?

Then I got mad at myself. I consider myself a somewhat intelligent person. After all, I had three years of college behind me. How come I never knew about the elusive Green Card? This went beyond clueless. It ranked high on the list of "Stupid!"

I never went back to the awning company. I didn't care how hot it got inside those houses when the sun shown in the windows.

On a brighter note, the Green Card became a moot point with me. A short time later I became a naturalized American citizen. So, I didn't ever need no stinkin' Green Card. Now, I am proud to say, "John Stephen Hrehovcik wears red, white and blue.

"You cannot teach a crab to walk straight."
Aristophanes

In his 1953 action western, *Hondo,* John Wayne
comes up to a youngster fishing in a small pond.
Wayne asks if he's catching anything. The youngster
says, "Not a bite." Then Wayne points out that the
sun is behind him casting a shadow on the water.

Wayne says, "If you can see your shadow so
can the fish. The other bank's the place." The
youngster tells Wayne his mother won't let him go
there because he can't swim. Wayne asks the
youngster how old he is.

He answers, "Six."

Wayne grabs the youngster by the scruff of
the neck and seat of his pants and flings him into the
pond. The boy lands in the water, screaming and
sinks like a rock star at end of his career. The boy

stays underwater for a few seconds, pops his head up, gulps for air, splashes around and sinks again. A few moments later he comes up for air swinging his arms and kicking his feet. This time he manages to keep his head above water. He swings and kicks some more. He starts to move forward. His swings become strokes and he makes it to the other bank. All excited, the youngster yells, "I did it! I did it!"

That's pretty much the way I taught my kids. I threw them into the pond and expected them to swim. One time, when Josh was about 10 and Noah 8, I decided to have them paint the garage door of the house we were building. I got out the paint, brushes, mixing sticks and rags and said, "Guys, I want you to paint the garage door. Do the best you can. I'll be back in an hour." I gave them some preliminary instructions, but pretty much left them on their own.

I had a business appointment that couldn't wait, got in my car and drove off. When I got back, the garage door had some paint on it, something like Tom Sawyer's whitewashed fence.

I used the Wayne technique on more occasions than I'd like to admit. I even refined it by having complex instructions just as I stepped out the door on my way to a meeting or some pressing appointment. I'd say something like, "Josh and Noah, take out the garbage, clean out the squirrels from the attic and find peace and harmony in the world." It took me a while to realize I wasn't John Wayne and my sons did not have roles in a movie.

I think I used this method for teaching my children because that's pretty much the way my father taught me. Watching and working with him in construction, I picked up working skills by osmosis, no real instructions. I figured this method would get the boys to think out problems, be creative and use their imaginations. Isn't this the way all fathers taught their children?

Of course, this method leaves a lot of room for unfortunate mistakes and missed opportunities. Worse, it plants the seeds of doubt and mistrust. I know that's what happened between my father and me. I stopped having confidence in him and didn't go to him when I had the kind of problems every growing kid has.

It took a while, but I learned the "throw 'em in the water" teaching technique had a major downside. While Josh, Noah and Gillian did learn to swim out of their problems, most of the time they learned without the comfort and encouragement they should have gotten with me to guide them.

Sure, I wanted them to become independent and self-reliant. But I know I missed out on an important part of being a parent – being there at a critical time when they needed me.

CHAPTER 12

THE CONSEQUENCES OF
THE UNEXPECTED

"It was a wine jar when the molding began: as
the wheel runs round why does it turn out a
water pitcher?"
Horace

Have you heard the yarn about Zeke and Albert on
their camping trip? After two weeks in a campsite
near a running stream they decide to head home.
They pack their gear and start to leave when Zeke
sees their campfire still blazing. Zeke says, "We'd
better put out that fire."

"Right," says Albert, "I'd get some water from
that stream, but I stowed away all my pots and pans."

"Don't worry." Zeke puts down his backpack.
"I'll make a basket out of some twigs." Zeke gathers
several twigs and branches and fashions them into a
rude basket. He goes to the stream and fills the basket
with water and goes back to the fire.

But by the time he reaches the fire all the water has drained out of the spaces between the twigs and branches. "Looks like you lost all your water," Albert observes.

Zeke grunts, returns to the steam and fills the basket again. "This time I'll run faster," says Zeke. With his basket refilled with water, Zeke double-times to the fire. But once again, all the water drains out.

Unfazed, Zeke returns to the stream, fills the basket with water and dashes full speed to the blazing fire. No luck. All the water drains out. He repeats refilling and dashing several times, only to have all the water gone by the time he reaches the fire.

"I guess this wasn't such a good idea," reflects Zeke.

"Well," Albert interjects, "At least you've got a clean basket."

This tale of Zeke and Albert serves as a metaphor for many ambitious attempts I made to solve one problem when an unexpected opportunity presented itself.

One of the best examples happened when I reconnected with a wonderful lady, Judith Hansen, a few years ago. In the early 1970s we worked at the *York County Coast Star*, the weekly newspaper that serves southern Maine. Judith wrote in the editorial department. I worked in advertising.

Over the years we both moved on. In 1992 she bought the *Tourist News,* a quality summer weekly providing vacationers and locals with happenings in the southern Maine area. Her vision and editorial skills kept the paper growing in popularity.

We bumped into each other in 2006 and I asked if she could use help with the paper. She said she needed someone to lay out the pages. With my newspaper and advertising experience it seemed like a natural fit.

I hadn't noticed in the years that passed by how much technology had passed by *me.* Judith used a computer program called InDesign to prepare each issue. This high-tech program makes it easy for a savvy computer person to arrange editorial stories, photos, advertisements and other newsworthy information in a readable and attractive format. Did I mention "savvy?"

While I had never worked with InDesign before, I figured "How hard can it be?" I did a crash course preparing a couple of issues. It didn't take me long to realize it was hard. It also didn't take long for Judith to realize the learning curve turned out to be too steep for me. She needed someone who worked faster.

Instead of struggling to learn InDesign, Judith asked me if I would be interested in writing an article for an upcoming issue. "Sure," said I, and switched from an InDesign wannabe to a much published freelance writer.

Since that first article, I have written more than 600 features for the *Tourist News*. With each article my confidence and resume grew. This led to other writing opportunities including *Travel Maine,* a major vacationer publication covering the state and several articles in *Discover Maine Magazine.* I also edited *YA-HA MOMENTS*, by Kathleen Allen, an original look at techniques for building sales, and *When There's No Wind, Row*, a personal memoir by Paula Singer. Singer's book described her remarkable struggle overcoming ingrained prejudice against women in the workplace. Enduring financial hardships, she earned her law degree, became a computer technology expert and an authority on international and national tax law. These editing experiences also provided me with material to teach several writing classes.

My baskets may have had holes in them, but every now and then they allowed a light to shine through on some unsuspecting and welcome surprise.

"True ease in writing comes from art not chance,
As those move easiest who have learn'd to dance."
Alexander Pope

In addition to learning the Pythagorean Theorem,
how to conjugate a verb and how we lost the Battle of
the Alamo, the administrators of my high school in
Linden, New Jersey, in the 1950s felt it important that
all students learn how to mingle in a responsible
manner.

Our enlightened school officials believed
education had more purpose than filling our heads
with details. They wanted the whole person to
prepare for life after high school. Students needed to
know how to handle themselves in social encounters.
In particular, with the opposite sex.

What more wholesome way to prepare us for
this moment of life transformation than to teach us
ballroom dancing. The teachers believed that dancing

75

with a partner would provide a number of learning experiences - such as coordination, maneuvering without crashing into somebody, keeping time to the music, and perhaps most critical, having a pleasant conversation with your partner while holding her.

So on the appointed day, rather than suit up in gym shorts and T-shirts, the boys were told to dress in a jacket and tie, the girls in party dresses. The boys lined up on one side of the gym, the girls on the other. Awkward tensions mounted as we eyed each other from across the gym floor.

The boys' coach, who turned in his whistle for dancing instructions, became Arthur Murray.

He commanded both boys and girls to find a random spot in the middle of the basketball court.

The coach said, "We are going to teach you the steps of a foxtrot. Boys, take a step forward with your left foot, then a step forward with your right. Now go sideways with your left foot, then bring your right foot next to your left. Got it?" It took a few clumsy attempts, but pretty soon we got it.

The girls' coach told the girls to do the same steps, only in reverse and backwards.

After most of us got that movement down with some level of confidence, we learned how to turn. Still without a partner.

All the while I concentrated on the steps, in the back of my mind I realized, with a bit of foreboding, I'm going to have to do this with a member of the opposite sex.

By my junior year in high school I had many friends who were girls, so I'm not sure why this particular dancing class caused so much anxiety. I'd attended dances before, even won a jitterbug contest, so I couldn't understand all the fuss that rattled around in my brain. Perhaps teaching us as a group made me feel awkward.

Once the coaches felt we had the steps under control, they told us to line up. Boys in one line, girls in another.

The coach said, "Boys, march forward until you are in front of a girl. She will be your partner."

This felt worse than picking sides on a baseball team. What if I wind up with someone I don't like, or is clumsy, or worse, what if I'm the one she doesn't like and I'm the clumsy one. I rubbed my hands against my pants to wipe the sweat oozing from my palms.

As it happened, my partner turned out to be a pretty girl I had never met before. She was a little taller than me, but not by much, so I hoped she didn't notice. She had red bouncy hair and a perky smile. I made the effort to be relaxed.

We got instructions where to put our hands. Her right in my left. My right hand on her waist. Her left hand on my shoulder.

The music began, so we began to dance. I asked her name. "Jenny," she said, "What's your name?"

I said, "Steve." It seemed like a good beginning.

She said she liked school and I could tell she was smart. Things were going rather well, I thought. We made a few smooth turns and managed to travel around the lines painted on the basketball floor without slamming into anyone.

Then there came kind of a lull in our conversation and I made an attempt to find a way to compliment her. So I said, "My, you're very big."

As soon as those words left my lips I could tell I made the biggest mistake of my life so far. There would be others.

Of course, I referred to the fact that she was taller than me. I had no intension of pointing out that she had rather sizable breasts, but I realized in that moment that's what she thought I meant.

She turned red and stiffened. I knew she misunderstood my gracious compliment. But there would be no way to undo those unkind words. Somehow we finished the dance, our eyes averting each other. When the music stopped, she rushed away.

We had to change dance partners every few dances until the end of the class. I didn't have the nerve to say anything to any of my new partners. They had their own nervousness to deal with, so they didn't seem to notice my lack of conversation.

I kept looking over my new partners' shoulders for Jenny, but couldn't find her. In fact, I'd never see her again. Not in any class or the halls or cafeteria. I don't think my harsh comment caused her to move away. It was just that our paths never crossed again.

Perhaps it was for the best. I doubt that I could think fast enough to salvage the damage.

I guess some things never have a proper ending. They just end. And we move on to the next blunder. In my case there would be many more.

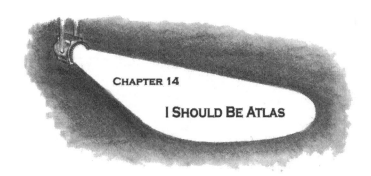

"That which does not kill us makes us stronger."
Friedrich Wilhelm Nietzsche

"Cowards die many times before their deaths;
The valiant never taste of death but once."
William Shakespeare

As I advance in my seventieth decade I have had the good fortune to avoid getting killed. So far. Fate or dumb luck? Who knows? Of course, as Shakespeare alludes, there are many kinds of deaths. With all the close calls and stupid mistakes, it's a miracle I survived. You'd think if Nietzsche can be believed, I'd be as strong as Atlas.

It may be a little unfair to judge myself as a coward. After all, doing a coward's deed requires some awareness of options. But in most of my exploits, I've been clueless about how to proceed. I don't know if I could count the many opportunities I've let slip by my attention.

One painful event stands out. To this day I get shivers thinking of what might have been.

While working at the bank in Cambridge in 1969, the musical *Come Summer* came to Boston for its pre-Broadway trial run. The show starred dancing legend Ray Bolger. My wife Carol and I went to see a matinee. While it had some delightful musical numbers and impressive performances, the production was a disaster. Theater buzz later told of backstage tensions among the actors, writers and directors that doomed any onstage magic. It was in such trouble when it got to Broadway it closed after only seven performances.

The musical's story about conflicted characters during the Civil War had a jumbled plot. On our ride home I kept reworking the story line. At last, I said to Carol, "I know what's wrong with the show and I can fix it." Carol humored me, the way she often did when I had an outrageous idea.

Feeling confident and emboldened by my story idea, when we got home I began to type out my solution to the story's problems. I wrote into the night and had completed my revisions to the plot and character development by morning.

The next day at work, I took my lunch break to time with the end of the show's matinee. I arrived backstage with the intention of speaking to the producer or writers. The stage door manager told me they were not around. Just then Ray Bolger came to the stage door.

Several people waited to get autographs. Bolger was very gracious and joking, even though he knew the Boston reviewers had panned the show.

After the other onlookers left I introduced myself to Bolger and complimented him on his performance. As we shook hands a thousand thoughts raced through my mind. Should I tell Bolger of my script improvements? Would it be more polite to wait and contact the producer or writers? What's the best way to say I could save the show without sounding impertinent?

Bolger saw my confusion and asked, "Anything else I can help you with?"

Tongue-tied and stumped, I mumbled, "No, thank you."

With that, Bolger strolled away, along with my dream of making Broadway history by saving a disastrous production.

Gone was my moment of glory as the unknown who transformed a hapless script. Lost was my fantasy of becoming the go-to guy to fix other Broadway shows in trouble. Vanished was my hope of having my picture on *Time* magazine as the "Theater Magician of the Year."

Of course, there could be no way to know if my revisions would have helped. Yet, to this day I regret I did all that rewriting and failed at the last moment to present it to Bolger. Who knows? He just might have considered my ideas worth exploring.

It's like I used to tell my kids when they almost finished a chore, "You hit a home run, but stopped on third base." It served as a painful lesson in not having enough confidence in myself.

This backstage encounter with Ray Bolger had an influence on future risky ventures. Not wanting to be guilty of allowing the possibility of a personal and financial triumph slip through my fingers, I'd attempt some outrageous ventures.

Like the time Carol and I took individual unsecured loans with a bank to finance a musical revue I wrote, produced and directed called *Round 'Bout Maine*. While I took great pride in the quality of the show, audiences didn't share my enthusiasm and declined to show up. In the unhappy tradition of *Come Summer*, I was forced to close when I couldn't meet the payroll.

This led to major financial troubles. Three lawyers recommended we declare bankruptcy. Carol and I just couldn't go through with the idea of not meeting our financial obligations. It took years, but somehow we managed to get our finances in order, thanks in the most part to Carol's careful purchasing and prudent bookkeeping.

Although my clueless handling of our finances forced us to lose the house we started to build in Kennebunkport, I look back on two personal triumphs at that time. When I designed the house, I made room for a fireplace. From the experience I gained working with my father in construction, I figured I could build the fireplace myself. I had never done it before, so I read several "How To" books.

It became a family project. Carol and the boys collected stones from around the yard while I mixed cement. I used the stones to create the fireplace inside. Working on a two-story scaffold, I built the stone chimney outside. It took several months and we celebrated when we finished. With a little trepidation, we piled logs into the hearth, lit some kindling and waited for the fire to blaze into life. It worked. The fire crackled and smoke rose up the chimney. It became one of our glowing achievements.

The second triumph consisted of my building all the doors in the house. Each one different with individualized trim and accessories. The door to the boys' room even had a small trap door, like an old speakeasy, to check who wanted to come in. I'm not sure if it was worth the effort, but somehow I seemed possessed to do it.

Perhaps Nietzsche got it right. All these disastrous experiences didn't kill me, and I guess I'm stronger in the way I go about looking at my life. I believe I can say with some confidence that I'm at least looking for the clues I now know present themselves in abundance. Often in plain sight, sometimes in unusual places. But they're there.

Where "muddle through" used to be my motto, now I'm better prepared with the strength and knowledge to meet what's coming. At quiet times when I'm not suspecting it, some painful memories grip my thoughts. But, only for a moment. Often I'd dispel their sting by saying to myself, "Look how much I've learned."

Of course, there are always more clues to discover. I don't think it's a stretch to say my rebellion has achieved some victories.

While not always according to any master plan, I bounced from one career to another searching to find some stability and purpose to my life. I'm proud to say I didn't just hang around hoping for good fortune to smile on me.

These days I enjoy my work as a freelance writer and artist. I've written more than 700 articles in vacation and travel publications and co-authored a movie script, *27 Down,* produced by an independent film company. I also had a short television series, *Bruce McToose, Intrepid Traveler,* shown on several stations. At the moment, I'm working on getting attention for several movie scripts and a Broadway musical comedy.

My artwork has won some modest awards and I've had commissions for portraits, Pen and Ink drawings of homes, equestrian and pet art and maps. I've had a lot of fun drawing cartoons, caricatures and illustrating several children's books. Two are eBooks, *Murfy Finds A Home* and *Murfy's River Adventure*, about a friendly mouse and lonely Grandpa Bob who become great pals.

I've also found great satisfaction using my art and writing experience, teaching drawing and writing classes.

So, I guess I can agree with Nietzsche. While nowhere near a match with Atlas, I've come out stronger by the many grim experiences I've had. I've managed to carry more weight on my shoulders and I can look back on many successes, often as the surprise development from other plans.

PART II
Getting A Clue

CHAPTER 15

HIDING IN PLAIN SIGHT

"... the lights burn low in the barber-shop
And the shades are drawn with care
To hide the haughty barbers
Cutting each other's hair."
Morris Bishop

When I returned to my car in the mall parking lot
not long ago I noticed that some Neanderthal had put
a dent in the back of my trunk. While not a serious
whack, it did blight the sleek look of my maroon 2003
Toyota Avalon.

Of course, there was no note under my
windshield wiper from the culprit with an abject
apology. No name. No address. More important, no
insurance company to contact for compensation. Just
the glaring dent.

While the dent annoyed me, it didn't impair
how the car drove. So, I figured I'd shrug the incident

91

off and drive on with the more important issues of my life.

Later, after a shopping spree with my wife Carol, I headed toward the car laden down with an armful of packages. I liked to put our bundles in the trunk instead of the back seat to avoid temptation by any hooligan passing by.

As I walked up to the car, I attempted to open the trunk the way I always did, by pushing the trunk button on my remote key ring. I fumbled with the packages to get my keys out of my pocket. I pushed the button. To my chagrin, the trunk that would obediently pop open with this electronic wizardry remained unmoved. Still fumbling with packages, my frustration growing, I opened the car, reached in and pushed the trunk button on my dashboard. Nothing.

Then I remembered the blatant attack on my trunk. I figured the hit had enough force to break the mechanism of the locking device. To open the trunk now I'd have to use the key. It felt so 1950s.

A short time later I took my wife to visit a friend. As luck would have it, her husband was a retired car mechanic. He loved to talk cars, so I showed him the dent in the trunk. I told him my sad tale about my lack of "button" power. He said, "Let's take a look."

He opened the trunk with my key and undid the inside covering. He found the trunk locking mechanism and showed me it had come apart. No doubt from the whack on the trunk. With a simple motion he connected the wires. He shut the trunk.

"Try it," he said. In great anticipation, I pushed the button on my remote. Miracle of miracles, the trunk popped open.

"How about the dashboard button?" I asked. I got behind the wheel and, all smiles, pushed the trunk button. Nothing. The trunk remained shut. My smile vanished.

"Oh well," I said, "at least the remote button works."

Of course, in the scheme of world affairs, how you opened your car trunk doesn't rank very high. Still, I stared at the button on the dashboard, pushed it now and again, with hopes it somehow would "heal" itself.

Several months later my son Josh needed to drive me somewhere, I'm not sure where. It doesn't matter. What matters is he got behind the wheel ready to drive off with me in the passenger seat.

Before he drove off, I opened the glove compartment looking for something. It doesn't matter for what. The glove compartment overflowed with papers, flashlight, auto manuals, a few books and sundry items - except gloves. I guess it's called a glove compartment as a holdover from the former days when drivers kept gloves there.

As I rummaged, Josh looked over and said, "What's this?"

From earlier conversations he knew of my frustration with the dashboard trunk button. I don't know how many times I opened the glove compartment, but I never saw it. It was another button. He pushed it. Then he pushed the trunk button on the dashboard. Another miracle of engineering, the trunk popped open.

I suppose this button in the glove compartment served as a security precaution to prevent unsavory valet parking attendants from getting into your trunk and stealing all your Christmas packages. I must have hit it by accident when reaching in for something. It doesn't matter for what.

Thanks to my alert son, who found the button in my glove compartment, I now had the option and pleasure of opening my trunk three ways - remote button, dashboard button and old reliable key.

That hidden button got me thinking. How many other "buttons of life" have I overlooked? The ones hidden in plain sight.

How many opportunities have I not seen, even though they screamed out at me? How many clues have I rebelled against rather than take advantage of the potential they offered?

Sometimes it takes someone else to help you see the obvious. Sometimes it takes a disaster or accident to make you realize what you did could have been smarter. History reveals examples of momentous discoveries that changed human destiny as the result of unintended consequences. Some significant, others rank as major conveniences.

Like the well-known account of Scottish scientist Alexander Fleming who discovered penicillin in 1929. While experimenting with a remedy for the flu virus he noticed one of the Petri dishes in his lab had become "infected" by a blue-green mold. The mold killed a bacteria growing in the dish. Voila! A cure for infections and many socially embarrassing diseases.

Or, how about the discovery of the microwave oven. In 1946 a Raytheon engineer, Percy Spencer, conducted tests in his lab with the kind of magnetrons that powered Allied radar in World War II. As he worked he felt a warm, oozy feeling in his pocket. To his amazement, he discovered the magnetron wave melted the chocolate bar in his pocket. Imagine. Now we have pizza in less than 4 minutes.

Let's not forget Velcro. Swiss engineer George de Mestral got annoyed when walking in the woods because burrs stuck to his socks and dog's fur. Under a microscope Mestral spotted small "hooks" that stuck to material. Years later he got the hooks to stick to nylon strips. So long zippers and shoelaces.

We celebrate such discoveries and inventions that lift our burdens. Yet, it's the prudent person who accepts how much of life remains complicated and unpredictable. Perhaps destiny intends for certain mysteries to challenge and strengthen us in our journey. The best we can do is to stay alert. We may discover a "button" to unlock some important clue hidden in plain sight.

CHAPTER 16

IT'S NOT HEAVY - IT'S MY BAGGAGE

"... a man must carry knowledge with him if he would bring home knowledge."
Samuel Johnson

Many people have traveled a lot more than me. But I guess I've tripped along to my fair share of destinations. Born on a small tobacco farm in Canada – yes, they grow tobacco in Canada – I moved with my family when I was two years old to New Jersey. Over the years I've also lived at various times in Florida, Illinois, Washington, D.C. and Massachusetts.

Either exhausted or exhilarated, or a little of both, in 1970 I moved my wife, Carol, and two sons, Joshua and Noah, to Maine where we decided to stay put. That's where our daughter Gillian was born.

Earlier, thanks to my service in the U.S. Army, my passport had stamps by the customs agents of several Far East countries. Sixteen months in South Korea introduced me to a culture of colorful kimonos, kimchi – a strong pungent staple of fermented, spicy vegetables that I couldn't get past my Western culinary bias – and some delightful people.

A couple of weeks in Japan seemed like a one giant visit to Disney World. In Thailand, as a souvenir I bought, what else, a tie. In Hong Kong I had a suit made in two days by a tailor who arranged for a chauffeur to give me a tour of this enchanted island. This puzzled me, since it wasn't an expensive suit. Growing a bit suspicious, I wondered if he sewed drugs or some secret code into the lining. Whenever I wore the suit I expected to be stopped by dubious characters who would rip off my clothes and run away with the secret cache.

When I finished my tour in South Korea I had hopes to travel by military hops back through the Middle East, Europe and then to my next U.S. assignment. I figured I traveled west halfway around the world. Why not continue my journey west to circumnavigate the globe?

I spoke to the U.S. Consulate in Okinawa about going to India next. He advised, "Don't go. You won't get out."

Probably one of the few pieces of advice I listened to. I didn't go to India. I returned to the states the normal way just in time not to be AWOL at Aberdeen Proving Ground in Maryland. There I completed my military service and re-entered the life of a domesticated civilian.

For all this traveling you'd think I would have figured out how to lighten my load. Of course, I'm not speaking of stuff I jammed into suitcases. That would be easy. No. My baggage is the kind I couldn't see and I had no clue weighed me down. I just kept lugging it around because I didn't have sense enough to unload it.

Perhaps the most burdensome weight that slowed me down came from an unwillingness to accept the fact that I didn't know everything. It's not that I thought I had a greater intelligence than others. I knew there were countless people smarter than me. It's just that I thought I had enough smarts to handle whatever I got into. And, what I got into most of the time was trouble. I took risks no sane person would attempt. For example, I started an advertising business with no clients, no capital and no plan. Just a lot of, as my Jewish friends might say, "Chutzpah!" Somewhere I picked up the notion if I worked hard, it would all work out fine. It would have helped if I worked smart.

I no longer embraced the biblical "Lilies of the Field" parable. Through many painful lessons I came to the conclusion I needed to do more than wave around like lilies to grow a fortune.

Like many hopeful shows heading for the Great White Way, my show closed out of town.

Accepting this fact, I cast off the idea of becoming a member of a Broadway cast. Painful, but I did it.

As anyone looking for a job knows, finding the right place to work is harder than doing the job. After numerous attempts, fortune at last smiled on me as the result of my joining a sales and marketing club. There I met Jerry Garman, the Sales Manager at Weyerhaeuser Paper Company in Westbrook. They manufactured corrugated packaging. He seemed to think my design work would be a good fit for the designer position they needed.

While I had no experience in packaging, I guess I showed enough design ability. I picked up what I needed to know on the job and it turned out to be a great job. It helped us get on a solid footing after so many financial upheavals in my erratic past.

Ever so slowly, I managed to shed some of my emotional baggage. The first difficult step came from accepting that I had baggage that weighed me down. One help came from listening to people who knew more than I did. To let in their wisdom was both humiliating and exhilarating at the same time.

With the help and encouragement of my patient wife Carol, I weighed my options before jumping into other dubious ventures. Maybe I modeled myself after a baseball player getting ready to face a challenging pitcher. The batter swings heavy bats to strengthen his swing. Could it happen that I bulked up my emotional muscles by lugging my weighty baggage all those formidable years?

Could I have done it easier? Sure.

Would I have? Probably not.

"He flattered himself on being a man without any prejudices; and this pretension itself is a very great prejudice."
Anatole France

There can be an upside to a lack of awareness. I don't recall becoming conscious of the word "prejudice" and the depth of its murky meaning until I reached high school. Even then it didn't seem to apply to me. Perhaps growing up in a section of Linden, New Jersey, called Tremley Point with a bunch of first generation immigrants got me immune to the idea of hating people because they have different backgrounds.

I tended to like some people because they had a friendly nature and disliked others because they were jerks. My preferences had nothing to do with ethnic background or skin color.

That's why I got a stunning "whack upside my head" about how ingrained prejudice had become in our culture. This revelation happened in a most unexpected place. It came when I had to give a class on U.S. Government to soldiers in my unit while stationed in South Korea.

By the time I entered the U.S. Army as a Reserve Officers' Training Corps 2nd Lieutenant in 1960 the military had become integrated. President Harry S. Truman started this controversial move in 1948. It took a painful period of adjustment, and some diehards couldn't shake their old bigoted beliefs. But for the most part, it seemed to be working. In my case, I had officers above me and enlisted men below me of color and it didn't make any difference. I had a two-year obligation on active duty and just wanted to get on with it without too much hassle.

As the newest 2nd Lieutenant in my company stationed just south of the Korean demilitarized zone, I got assigned to a variety of duties no one else wanted. Some gave me more satisfaction than others, like coordinating help for the local orphanage and organizing the movie schedule at the officers' club. When my captain learned I had a passing knowledge of U.S. history he assigned me to teach the class that would have a profound effect on me.

The class would cover the three branches of the Federal Government – Executive, Legislative and

Judicial. I had a pretty good grasp on how they worked – or didn't, depending on the political forces in play at the time. As I planned how to present the class I knew giving a lecture would not work. The soldiers in the class would be asleep before I got through "We the People ..."

With my theater background I had to think of something more dramatic, more memorable. I figured to make the most meaningful impression I had to get everyone to participate.

So, when the time for the class arrived I mounted the classroom stage and faced my victims. The class consisted of about 50 enlisted men. Many were colored. I'm not sure what the rest were. I knew most had completed high school, but may not have had much familiarity with U.S. history. In my best booming stage voice, I introduced my subject: "Gentlemen. Today we will learn about the three branches of government."

You could hear the rolling of eyes and see the moans of ennui ripple through the audience. Undeterred, I pressed on. "There are three branches of government and in order to demonstrate how they work you all will become part of this experiment." A few heads perked up.

I pointed to a group on the left side of the audience. "You 12 men come up on the stage. Bring your chairs and sit down over there. Let's snap it up."

After a few grumbles they picked up their chairs and assembled on the stage.

I spread my arms over the group and said, "You are the Legislative Branch. There are two parts. You four over here are the Senate. You other eight are the House of Representatives." As I explained there are two senators from each state and the number in the house depends on the state's population, the soldiers seemed to get into the spirit of the game. It looked like this participation approach just might work.

Bolstered by my success so far, I pointed to nine more soldiers in the audience. "Come up on the stage. You will be the Justices of the Supreme Court. Don't forget your chairs. Sit on the other side." As they came up I heard one say with a smile in his voice, "Hey, here comes da judge." They settled in their chairs and I told them they represented the nine justices and they made decisions about the constitutionality of laws Congress passed. They had their office for life. A few nodded their heads. They liked this idea. I went into a few details about how they were selected by the President and approved by the Senate, but I didn't get in too deep.

So on stage right I had the Congress and stage left the Supreme Court. I sensed the class was going well. All I needed was the President. I looked out into the audience and singled out a gruff-looking soldier. "Come on the stage with your chair."

106

He realized everyone was watching, so he grabbed his chair and sauntered up on the stage.

"Sit in the middle," I said. He plunked his chair on the floor and sat down.

With a dramatic inflection to emphasize the importance of the position, I said, "Here he is, gentlemen, the President of the United States."

As soon as I said those words a stunned silence flooded the room. Everyone looked around with a puzzled look as if waiting for some explanation. It took me a few moments to realize what caused this curious reaction. Then I noticed it. The President of the United States of America was a black man.

I'm not sure what went on in the minds of these soldiers turned politicians in my class. But I have no doubt some wondered, "Could it be possible for a black man to become the President? Of America?"

Others may have thought, "Not in my lifetime." Or, "We'd have to be a different country." Or, "They'd never let it happen."

Some may even have imagined, "Hey, maybe it could be me."

Even though I didn't intend for it to be part of my lesson plan, I could tell from their reaction for one brief moment I gave them a large dose of a dream to consider. Their low expectations had become so entrenched it would take a miracle to change their limiting attitude.

The class continued with me droning on for a short while, but no one seemed to be listening. They couldn't get beyond the preposterous idea that a Negro could be elected President. I dismissed the class and like it often happens, the teacher learns more from the students than they learn from him.

I came away from the class with a new insight. For all the blessings we enjoy in America, we also have atrocious chapters in our history. So many have suffered from laws and traditions created by narrow minds. I guess we're making progress, but imagine what our short-sighted prejudice has cost us.

As the years passed, courageous men and women have broken through barriers and opened new possibilities for those who follow. Today, people of all colors and backgrounds have more advantages than ever before. Many have outstanding careers in sports, business, medicine, the entertainment world and other high profile arenas. Even politics.

Perhaps skin color may become no more important than if you're a blonde, have hazel eyes or are six feet tall. It just won't matter, except as a way to describe our distinctions. We'll connect with those who seem friendly and avoid them when they act stupid.

I have no clue what happened to that soldier who sat in the President's chair in my class. I did notice, for a moment, he sat a bit taller.

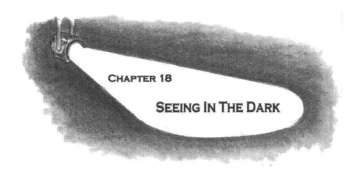

"A day without sunshine is like ... night"
Steve Martin

"It is at night that faith in light is admirable."
From *Chantecler* by *Edmond Rostand*

When you're presented with a clue that can change your life for the better, it's helpful if you pay attention. Over the years my attention span proved erratic. Often after I looked into my life's rearview mirror I realized I was given a clue that would help me. It's ironic that one of the clues that would shed some significant light on my view of life happened in the pitch dark.

I got this clue when I joined with a cadre of boisterous soldiers during Army training at Fort Benning, Georgia. We gathered in an auditorium as part of a "Night Training Course." We faced a lone instructor who paced on the bare stage. He carried a flashlight which he blinked at us.

"Gentlemen," his voice boomed with an authority that caused us to quiet down. "Tonight we will put your night vision to an extreme test." He paced left, then right, all the while flashing the light into the audience. "You will notice," he continued, "that the auditorium lights are beginning to dim. This will help your eyes become accustomed to the dark." Sure enough the room grew darker bit by bit. "Even the exit lights will be extinguished," he spoke as he continued to pace back and forth. All the while he passed the glow of his flashlight across the audience.

"Once we are in total darkness," he went on, "I will pace back and forth to the left and right. You are to yell out in which direction I move."

It looked like it might even be fun.

Ever so slowly the auditorium got darker and darker. As he promised, the exit light went out. At last, total darkness surrounded us. I remember holding up my hand in front of my face. I'm sure it was there, but I couldn't see it. Through the darkness the only thing visible was the bright glow from the flashlight.

"Okay," the instructor asked, "In which direction am I moving? Yell it out."

The instructor walked to the right. I called out, "To the right." He moved the light to the left. I called out, "Left." Back and forth the instructor strolled with the light and we called out the direction. I thought, "What's so hard about this?"

That's when it got bizarre. I saw the light move right again, so I yelled out, "Right." But the guy in the seat next to me yelled out, "Left!"

I thought this guy was crazy. Then some other soldier a couple seats away called out "Left." Meanwhile, around the auditorium in absolute darkness others called out with added conviction "Left!" "Right!" - with even more sincerity and volume "Right!" "Left!"

Then the light moved straight up. "Oh, he's getting tricky," I thought, but I'm on to him, so I yelled out, "UP!" But others didn't agree. "Left!!!" "Right!!!" "Up!!!" "Down!!!" By now the noise in the auditorium started to rival a rock concert.

The light kept shifting, up, down, right, left, sideways, forward, back. "Left!" "Right!" we yelled. "Up!" "Down!" Louder and louder. Each man convinced he knew what he saw.

And then it happened.

Someone switched on the auditorium lights. The brightness flooded the room followed by a thousand soldiers stunned into an eerie silence. For on the stage we saw the unbelievable. Our brains raced to make sense of it. Hanging securely on the

113

rung of an "A" frame ladder, like a lighthouse beacon, an unmoving flashlight shined out at us.

But where was the instructor? We found him twenty-five feet away. He leaned against the right wall of the stage, arms crossed, a knowing look of satisfaction on his face. The look told us he had made his point.

At the speed of thought an inconceivable idea raced through our minds. What we thought we saw, what we believed with unshakable conviction, the image we would have fought for was 100% wrong. Our instincts struggled to refute it. Impossible as it seemed, we realized that the flashlight never moved.

But how could that be? We "saw" the light move. "Left," "Right," "Up," "Down." We would each swear to it as an undeniable fact.

Then reality set in. We understood that the erratic movement of the light we "saw" was a phenomenon in our imagination. Our minds played a devious trick on us.

It went beyond sobering. For this was more than an experiment in night vision. This experiment with a flashlight in the dark would challenge my very belief system to the core. Should I believe something just because I swear I witnessed it? Can I base my convictions on what I think I observed? Is what I "see" truly what occurred?

On some level, which I would not appreciate for some time, I got a clue about another dimension of human understanding. I would learn to appreciate that this experience in the dark was not unique with me. Others could be just as guilty of a faulty belief system. Like me, in spite of their sincere convictions, they could be wrong.

This led me to realize that I needed to be patient with people who expressed their passionate beliefs. Their convictions are built on the way they see their life's experiences. Perhaps they see their light through their mental prism moving left or right or up or down. And maybe it *is*. Or maybe it is standing still and they choose to see it moving.

It took years to appreciate this clue, but it eventually taught me to become more tolerant and a better listener. I also learned that it was inappropriate to try to force someone to agree with me. After all, I could be wrong. By the same token, someone trying to convince me of their views, regardless of their fervor and confidence, could be wrong as well.

So where do we go from here? If everybody's beliefs are on shaky ground, how can we find what is true and real? How can we discover a way to live and work together when so many conflicting opinions abound?

Perhaps the clue is we can only be certain of uncertainty. And so rather than force others to agree with us, we work to find a common bond amongst us.

115

Rather than coercing others, we find a way to be willing to accept another point of view.

Perhaps then we'll let someone else shine their light into our darkness. In like manner, we can brighten their gloom. If we accept that no one of us can know enough, we will all be better off when we help each other.

I wish I had learned this clue earlier. It would have saved me from stumbling around in my invented darkness.

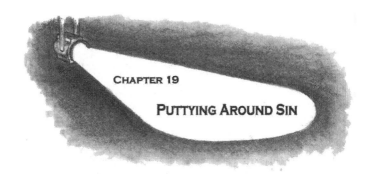

CHAPTER 19

PUTTYING AROUND SIN

Neither do I condemn thee: go, and sin no more.
Bible: John 8:11

Imagine that you exist as a fine sheet of oak wood.
You have a high polish so all the grains appear in
clear, distinct patterns. No knotholes, no scratches,
just an immaculate board of lumber. It would be
perfect for a skilled craftsman to fashion into an
elegant piece of furniture or home decoration.

This stylish sheet of oak represents you at
your most pure and innocent. Yet, in an unexpected
moment of weakness or by conniving circumstance
you experience a troublesome mistake. Life has given
you a moment of decision and you selected a
dishonorable path. Perhaps you even commit what
some would call a sin. You could say your offense
took the shape of a rusty nail that got hammered into
your pristine oak panel.

After a short time you realize your mistake, feel remorse and acknowledge your so-called sin. With this admission the nail gets pulled out from the board. What a good feeling not to have that offending nail burrowed into your smooth, clear board.

But all is not well. For the board has a cavernous hole remaining where the offending nail pierced the wood. The hole becomes a gapping gulch that mars your beauty. It remains as a constant reminder of your transgression. No matter how beautiful the rest of your board looks, you cannot ignore that hole. It taunts you with the memory of how you failed.

What can you do? Is there some way to deal with this intruding disagreeable memory?

Allow me to offer a solution I discovered to help ease any discomfort. It may seem silly, but it works.

In fact, it is silly, because it's putty. You know how much fun you can have with putty. You knead it so it's soft and pliable. Then you can create different forms like puppet faces, cars or other playful objects.

In the case of your blemished oak board, with delicate fingers you fashion the putty into a supple mass, find the hole in your board and fill it. The board becomes smooth again. With some clever adjustments you can arrange for the color of the putty to match the shade of the board. The hole and its memory no longer offend you, because you have forgiven yourself and you become smooth and beautiful again.

But you say, "I'm not a piece of oak wood, I'm a person."

Of course, you are.

But like that wood with the rusty nail, who hasn't made a mistake, done something stupid or even committed a serious offense – legal or otherwise?

And like that rusty nail, even if removed, hasn't the hole caused pain and hardship? Perhaps sleepless nights, or worse. While it's easy to see how putty works on the oak board, is there something that would have the same healing effect in our lives?

Somewhere I learned that the mind cannot hold two conflicting ideas at the same time. You can switch with lightning speed from one to the other, but not two simultaneously. It's humanly impossible.

This becomes the solution. Fill the hole with a memory that reminds you of happy, glorious, successful times.

It may help to find a mantra or positive saying the moment you get burdened with the hurtful memory. Once you start to fall into that hole, catch yourself and say something like, "It's a beautiful day," or "I'm a lucky person," or take a breath and count to ten. Anything that gets your mind off that offending hole. Fill it with uplifting thoughts.

As this book of clueless events in my life shows, my oak board has been riddled with rusty nail holes. While I've filled them with my form of putty, sometimes the putty slips out and I have to refill the hole.

Life is nothing else if not memories. The beauty of memories is you pick the ones you'd rather relive. I'll bet for every rusty nail in a life, there exists many more rainbows, majestic sunsets and personal triumphs.

Keep your putty handy. You never know when you'll knead it.

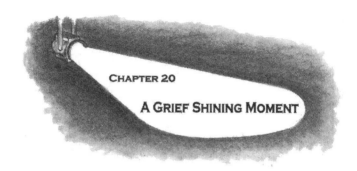

"I'm gonna make him an offer he can't refuse."
Vito Corleone in the film "The Godfather"

When I traveled to Chicago in search of theater work
I had the good fortune to have cousins on my
mother's side who lived in the south end of the city.
They were kind enough to allow me to stay with them
while I made the rounds for a job. We all hoped it
wouldn't last too long.

When I explained my plight to one cousin he
offered to help. He told me he was active in the local
political party and boasted he had some connections.
He said, "I don't know much about theater, but I
know Chicago. The city has an active arts and crafts
program. Maybe I can check out what they have in
one of the city-sponsored theatre districts."

This sounded like good news. He made a few
phone calls and arranged an interview for me with the
woman who ran the city's arts program. Could the

answer to my dreams to work in the theater start out this easy? Filled with high hopes, I went to meet her. She seemed very encouraging and said she had several possibilities in the city's summer programs for a young, eager theater person like me.

Everything seemed set. All I needed was a reference from some city official. Not knowing any city official, I went back to my cousin, who seemed to know his way around such affairs.

"No problem," he said. A couple of days later he took me to meet a man who served as an officeholder in the local district.

We chatted for about ten minutes. Me, all eager and enthusiastic. Him, listening and looking me up and down. I told him about my dream of working in Chicago's summer theater program, but in order to get the job, I needed a city official to sponsor me.

To my amazement, after this short conversation, he went to his typewriter and dashed off the most glowing letter of recommendation. It was beautiful. It almost embarrassed me. He claimed he knew of my superior qualifications and how industrious I was and how I can use my theater experience to make a valuable contribution to the summer theater program of Chicago.

For sure this letter would help me launch my theatrical career. What luck!

Or was it?

After reading the letter to myself a couple of times I got this strange queasy feeling in my stomach. Something just didn't sit right.

Mind you, this experience took place years before the film *The Godfather*. Yet, some instinct told me if I used this letter to get the theater job, one day I would have to repay this politician. I just met him 10 minutes ago. I had no idea who he was, what he stood for, or what future demands he would make on me. What offer would he make that I couldn't refuse?

Still, it could mean the difference between getting that dream job, or walking the streets, searching. I agonized about what to do. Do I use the politician's phony letter or take the high moral ground?

Maybe I just wasn't ready for this kind of complication in my life. Or, maybe I had serious reservations about becoming embroiled with someone who seemed suspicious. Was this the way Chicago politics works? Or was it just how politics everywhere works? I was definitely out of my league.

I never used the letter. I never went back to see the woman in charge of Chicago's arts program and I never learned what happened to the politician.

Did I make the right decision? I'll never know. Perhaps I should have trusted my cousin. I don't think he would have put me in jeopardy. But I couldn't shake the insincerity of the politician's letter.

Perhaps the politician just wanted to help out a struggling actor. Could he have had the best of intentions and all he may have wanted was front row seats when I made it big?

I don't have a clue if I was a jerk for missing out on a golden opportunity. Or did I save myself from a calamitous entanglement with a corrupt political system?

Some decisions will always remain a mystery.

CHAPTER 21

IT'S ALL GLEN CAMPBELL'S FAULT

"Lave us take some iv th' blame ourselves."
Finley Peter Dunne

"Some praise at morning what they blame at night;
But always think the last opinion right."
Alexander Pope

In times of trouble, one of the best ways to cope with the misery we face is to find someone to blame. While it happened a bit after the fact, I've discovered the person responsible for many of the murky quandaries I'd gotten myself into.

The culprit is none other than Glen Campbell. What a relief. I could pin all the clues I missed on singer Glen Campbell.

In 1967 Glen Campbell recorded the song "By the Time I Get to Phoenix." It became a major hit. It won two Grammy awards and reached #2 on

127

the U.S. Country Charts. At first blush this indictment may seem somewhat harsh. But think of the song's significance.

The lyrics tell the story of a guy who is faced with a heart-wrenching dilemma. He's decided to desert the woman he's been living with. But he hasn't got the guts to face her to tell her he's leaving. So he sneaks out while she's sleeping and leaves a damn note on the door. He figures he'll have gotten as far as Phoenix by the time she wakes up and finds the note.

He imagines her thinking the note may be a joke because he's left her before. From what he says, she's the one who works, and no doubt supports him. It's not like he had a job, since he just up and leaves. No two weeks' notice to his boss from this leech.

By now he's getting farther and farther away, high tailing it all the way to Albuquerque. Not convinced the note he left is real, the woman gives him a call at the house. No answer. It's late at night. She's tossing in bed, crying on the pillow. It's beginning to dawn on her the creep is really gone. Meanwhile he's made tracks all the way to Oklahoma.

When the song ends we've witnessed the end of a relationship that was doomed before it started.

Here is the picture of a good-for-nothing lowlife who can't face up to the responsibility of being a man. A sneak, a parasite, a coward.

So why are all my troubles Glen Campbell's fault? Because Campbell's rendition of the song and the sorry story it tells touched a nerve in my psyche.

It may seem strange that I blame Campbell for my troubles. After all, many of the stupid choices I made happened long before he recorded the song.

A valid point.

However, upon hearing the song, I began to realize its theme of escape and unwillingness to face some harsh realities was not far from my story. Campbell was singing about me. And it was not a pretty picture.

There's another reason I feel justified to blame Campbell. It comes from my life's ambition to play the piano. I took lessons in school, had a private teacher, watched piano videos and practiced, practiced, practiced. In spite of all that effort I never got beyond a fair rendition of "Chopsticks."

This all changed when my piano teacher gave me the sheet music for "By the Time I Get to Phoenix." I sat down at the piano, opened the sheet music and played as if I performed at Carnegie Hall. Flawless, with a spiritual quality. How this happened I have no clue. Carol, who happened to be in the next room, came over to me and said, "I've never heard you play so beautifully. It sounded so emotional and soulful." I never played it as well again.

Is this a stretch to connect with Campbell? Perhaps. But, to me, it makes sense on some level, so I'm sticking to it.

Some say it's only a song. What's the big deal?

Consider what Percy Bysshe Shelley said: "Poets are the unacknowledged legislators of the world." Poets don't just make pretty rhymes. They make history. The essence of poetry rises above mere stringing descriptive words and phrases together. Their magical arrangements of ideas reach into our hearts and reveal the substance of our being. They help us make sense of the world in a way no other art form can. They can arouse our imagination and motivate us with the courage and strength to deal with complex events and relationships.

Today the poets of Shelley's days have been replaced with the writers of lyrics to popular songs. With the success of Campbell's interpretation of "Phoenix" I got an inkling of my own shortcomings. It unnerved me to think I could be so shallow and unaware. In a sense Campbell's recording gave men like me permission to be irresponsible.

No doubt others identified with the song's message and made it so popular. Small comfort that I fit in with such a miserable crowd who sidestepped mature actions and dependability.

Perhaps Jimmy Webb, who wrote the lyrics and music, should share some of the responsibility.

But several other singers recorded the song and none had the impact of Campbell.

One glimmer of hope consoles me that I never gave up. I recall my experience when I saw *South Pacific* as a teenager in high school. The uplifting music of Rodgers and Hammerstein influenced me to pursue a life in the theater. While that pursuit had its difficulties, it led to some rewarding moments as well, discovering meaningful relationships, satisfying careers and new places to live.

At least Campbell's rendition helped shed some light on why I hit a raft of speed bumps, crashed into detour signs and drove over a few cliffs.

In spite of all those calamities, somehow I survived. Maybe I wasn't a total loss.

FEE-NIX

132

CHAPTER 22

SOUR NOTES AND
FADED JEANS

"How sour sweet music is
When time is broke and no proportion kept!
So is it in the music of men's lives."
William Shakespeare

"Oh! ever thus, from childhood's hour,
I've seen my fondest hope decay;
I never loved a tree or flower
But 'twas the first to fade away."
Thomas Moore

When I was about eight years old I often passed a music store with an accordion in the window. It was a real accordion, not a toy, but built smaller to fit a child's hands. The keys were shiny and the case had a colorful decoration that sparked my young imagination. I looked at that accordion and my head spun with the idea of the fun it would be to create music on it.

Somehow, I got up the courage to ask my father if he would get me that accordion. At my young age, I had no idea how much the accordion cost or how my father could pay for it.

My father worked two jobs to support our family. He was industrious, but there was little extra for frivolous items like a child's accordion. I guess he could see the disappointment in my eyes when he said he couldn't buy it.

To my great surprise, a short time later he bought me an accordion. But it wasn't the accordion in the window I longed for. It was a toy, plastic accordion. I looked at the accordion in despair. I felt crushed and cheated.

I don't think I ever played that toy accordion. I have no way of knowing for sure, but I have a suspicion that my father was disappointed with me, because I wouldn't even give it a try.

This experience may have even set the tone of the strained relationship between my father and me. To this day I have no clue if my father couldn't afford the real accordion or if he just didn't think I would play it. Sad to say, when I'd become a father I'd relive this painful experience.

Flash forward many years to the time I took my ten-year-old daughter, Gillian, shopping for jeans. Big mistake. What did I know about girl's jeans?

We visited a clothes shop that specialized in young girl's clothing. She spotted the jeans she liked. No, she loved them. She tried them on, they fit perfectly and she looked terrific in them. Then I checked the price tag. $29.95. I'm sure the shock on my face registered with both Gillian and the lady clerk. Remember this was years ago, before $200 jeans were the fashion norm.

Not only did I not have enough money to buy the jeans, my quick calculations told me it would be a big mistake to buy those jeans. At the time my finances could be described as "in ruins." My mortgage was two months overdue. The advertising business I started on a whim had yet to make any serious income. I was driving a used car that broke down with the phases of the moon. I didn't have a credit card. I didn't even know where or when I'd get my next paycheck.

Gillian looked up at me with expectation in her eyes. The clerk looked at me wondering how I could refuse buying my daughter the jeans she loved.

Agony! How could I justify paying so much money for jeans she'd probably wear twice and grow out of. But how could I disappoint her?

Back and forth I went, pitting the practical knowledge that I just didn't have enough money against my desire not to disappoint my dear daughter. Gillian and the clerk waited the eternity as I weighed the possibilities.

I never connected my disappointment of not getting the accordion with those cursed jeans. So, to my utter regret my practical side won. But my fatherhood and self-esteem lost. I didn't get the jeans. We left the store. Both of us felt abysmal. It was one of my most painful memories.

I now realize I should have begged, borrowed, maybe even stolen the money. Anything to keep from disappointing Gillian. Perhaps if I had more faith in myself I would have known that somehow I'd get back on my financial feet.

But at the time I was in a downward moral and spiritual spiral. It would take a climb up Mount Everest to regain some semblance of self-respect and forgiveness. Who would think there'd be a father's generational connection between a child's accordion and fashion jeans?

CHAPTER 23

SAGAS OF FAILURE
HAVE AN ALLURE

"Here lies one who meant well, tried a little,
failed much: surely that may be his epitaph, of
which he need not be ashamed."
Robert Louis Stevenson

Two unrelated items have a link that exposed a flaw
in my Achilles' emotional heel and caused me to
stumble much too often.

Both demonstrate my curious fascination with
failed causes. Somehow in my meandering journey I
came to embrace two conflicting belief systems. In
one, I accepted as an undeniable fact that I didn't
deserve to achieve success. In the other, all I had to
do was show up, and with the least amount of effort,
I'd triumph in all I attempted. As a way to reconcile
these clashing points of view I found a comfort in
learning about disastrous events. Perhaps I needed to
understand how others dealt with their failures in

order to help me overcome obstacles I knew I would face.

One item concerned the massive engineering project to build the Panama Canal by the French canal company, La Société Civile Internationale du Canal Interocéanique. Construction started in 1881, but the project ended eleven years later in failure and disgrace.

The other example of a fiasco is depicted in the 1991 film, *The Commitments*. The plot follows the exploits of a driven promoter in Dublin, Ireland, who forms a musical group. Each musician has talent, but their personalities clash. Yet, their music brings in larger crowds with each engagement. As the story unfolds, the musicians grow hostile and suspicious of one another. On the verge of a major discovery by a talent scout, they destroy any chance of success.

I became intrigued with the French attempt to build the Panama Canal as a result of a college term paper research assignment. My college professor instructed us to find any relevant topic that caught our imagination and to write a detailed report about it.

I'm not sure why I picked the Panama Canal. In fact, I could have written about the canal's successful completion by the United States in 1914. At the time it ranked as the engineering marvel of the world that connected the Atlantic and Pacific Oceans. Instead, in keeping with my unconscious belief that I was not worthy, I identified with the debacle by the French.

My research introduced me to Count Ferdinand de Lesseps, the celebrated architect who built the Suez Canal that opened in 1869. This success gained him financial and political support to build the canal in Panama.

But disaster loomed. They made mistakes in estimating the volume of earth they needed to excavate. The unpredictable rainy season caused massive landslides. Yellow fever, cholera, malaria and other diseases depleted crews. Behind the scenes political maneuvering, bribes to bankers, conflicts with the press and private interests all contributed to major time delays and massive cost overruns.

When the project ended in bankruptcy in 1889, it brought financial ruin to thousands of investors and the once revered name of de Lesseps became synonymous with corruption and scandal.

The more I researched, the more fascinated I became in the gigantic scope of the failure.

In the film *The Commitments,* the disaster occurred on a more modest level. Just a bunch of musicians who didn't make the big time. Perhaps, the entertainment value of the music drew me in and I paid less attention to the impending doom taking place before my eyes.

Nevertheless, the failure of de Lesseps and *The Commitments* resonated with me. There was a measure of comfort for me. If something as real as the Panama Canal and the make-believe story of a movie could demonstrate such a failed experience, maybe it was okay for me to do the same.

Can you imagine the twisted logic that justified this rationale? This fascination with failure reveals why so many of my dreams turned into nightmares, among them losing our home, teetering on bankruptcy and threatening my marriage.

Perhaps my rebellious streak saved me. Something inside said don't give in to the temptation to give up.

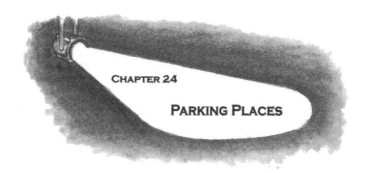

"No Parking"
A Street Sign

You don't have to drive into downtown Boston on a Friday night to search for a place to park. It could happen in a mall parking lot or any side street. Is it possible that when you can't find a parking place the cosmos is sending you a message? Is the lack of parking places a secret code encouraging you to move on to more spacious pastures?

Quite by accident I learned a great lesson from my car. It's a lesson I wish I had heeded much earlier in my life. It's not like I hadn't been given a number of clues along the way. Had I paid attention I could have avoided many a disaster.

I discovered the lesson when I promised to take my wife Carol to dinner. Going out to dinner is one of Carol's favorite events. I hoped to impress her with my thoughtfulness. It was Friday night and we picked the restaurant with care. Though we had never been to this restaurant before, it had excellent reviews. Both of us looked forward to a wonderful, relaxing evening.

As we approached the restaurant we felt reassured it would live up to its reputation because the parking lot was full. This was a good sign. A full parking lot means people approve. Our expectations rose even higher.

I pulled into the lot and searched for a spot. No opening in the first row so I circled around to the next area. Nothing there either. Maybe I'd find something on the street. But first I circled around the lot again. Every spot was taken. Okay, let's try around the corner.

Oh, good, I found a spot. I pulled up. Damn! A fire hydrant. I drove away and searched down a side street. By then we started to lose our appetites. Carol saw a space on the other side. It was tight, but I squeezed the car in.

We got out of the car and walked the two blocks to the restaurant. Once in the restaurant we got in line for a table. The wait wasn't too long and we tried to laugh off the lack of parking space. We got our table where the waitress wasn't having a great night. Carol doesn't take kindly to petulant waitresses, so when the food finally came she wanted it to taste great. Well, it was awful. Cold and bland.

We both realized this was a big mistake. We struggled through the meal with the idea of getting it over with as quickly as possible and leaving. We trudged back to the car feeling miserable.

Once in the car Carol looked at me and pointed out that when we couldn't find a good parking spot right off we should have left. She wanted to say something sooner but knew when I was determined to do something there was no stopping me, no matter what complications stood in my way.

It was the challenge for me that I had to conquer. This had become my trademark. I face the dragons and slay them. The challenge of finding a parking space was like Lancelot discovering the Holy Grail.

I don't know how I got the clue, but I began to realize some goals, no matter how alluring, just weren't worth the extra effort. Maybe it was the sad look on Carol's face. Maybe not finding a parking place, waiting in the long line, the poor service, the unappetizing meal. Everything added up to a disaster.

From that moment, when obstacles appeared, we'd ask, "Is this a parking place?"

CHAPTER 25

IT AIN'T NECESSARILY, SOW

"Sow a thought, and you reap an act;
Sow an act, and you reap a habit;
Sow a habit, and you reap a character;
Sow a character, and you reap a destiny."
Anonymous quote by Samuel Smiles

"The more we arg'ed the question the more we didn't agree."
Will Carleton

With all my changing jobs on a whim, searching for pots of gold at the end of fading rainbows and making surprise decisions on a wild impulse, you might expect that Carol and I had a few disagreements. Some were larger than others. Some were HUGE.

A typical example occurred when our son Joshua told me he wanted to quit school. He just entered his senior year in high school and hated it. I appreciated his dilemma. I figured he was smart enough to learn what he needed to know to make his mark on the world without the formal structure of a classroom. So I sided with him. Carol couldn't disagree more. With her teaching experience, she understood what a mistake it would be for Joshua to quit when he was so close to graduating.

Carol and I went round and round about what would be the best for Joshua. We both knew the value of a good education. But, would continuing in school while he disliked being there make it difficult for him to learn anything? Or should he tough it out and make the best of it while he got his high school degree? No matter how much we discussed it, we couldn't agree.

It took some outside help for us to decide. At the time Joshua was seeing a counselor to help him cope with some personal issues. When Carol and I told the counselor about the problem, he said, "Make him finish high school. If he doesn't, he'll regret it the rest of his life."

I didn't agree with the counselor and told him how unhappy Joshua was going to school. The counselor pointed out he knew Joshua always brought his books home, did his homework and got good grades. He was sending us a mixed message which was too subtle for me to grasp.

I held my ground thinking Joshua needed someone on his side. Then the counselor said,

"You're paying me good money for my advice. Take it." Then he looked me straight in the eyes and said. "Steve, you must be the one to tell Joshua. Not Carol."

Oh, boy. This meant I had to backtrack. As difficult as it was for me, I realized Carol was right. I told Joshua he had to finish. I knew he felt I let him down, but I guess deep down I wanted him to finish high school. As much as he didn't like it, he trudged back to his classes. He graduated with honors. Go figure.

Another time Carol and I had a major difference of opinion occurred when I came home all excited about a new idea. While strolling on the beach I received what I considered a vision from on high. It seemed like a spiritual moment. We had just started construction of our new home in Kennebunkport and I felt pressure to find a source of income. With the sand curling between my toes, my hands buried in my pockets, my eyes searching the water for a sign, any sign, it came to me: I'll start a theater! Brilliant, I thought. How many times have I read about inspiration that came at unsuspecting moments of deep inner reflection that turned into a startling success?

A theater. It's what I always wanted. The fact that I had no money, no place to put it, no backing, no plan to carry it out were all minor details that I'd work out. How hard could it be? If I believed I could do it, I'd get it done – somehow. That's what I learned from every motivational book I read.

Filled with bubbling enthusiasm I rushed home to share my discovery with Carol. Maybe I didn't set it up right, because before I could get beyond "I want to start a theater," Carol said, "NO!"

I couldn't believe it. No discussion. No, let me explain. No, wait until you hear how great it will be. Carol had enough. She had reached her limit with my brainy ideas. She said, "If you want to build a theater, go ahead. But, it won't be with me."

I could tell by the sound of her voice and look in her eyes there was no room for negotiating. It was like a combined Mohammad Ali punch to my stomach and a bowling ball dropped on my foot.

More than any physical pain, I felt emotionally shattered. Carol, who always went along with my wildest notions, rebelled. I had no clue why. It took me a while to accept her decision, which I admit made more sense than my wild dream. You'd think I had learned my lesson from all my previous disasters. Some people have a hard time accepting reality.

Which points out the lesson we both learned from incidents like Joshua wanting to quit school and me dreaming (perhaps I should say hallucinating) about starting a theater. We realized it wasn't those specific events that put us at odds. It was a question of who decides and why. When enough time passed so we could get over the hurt feelings, we discovered one of the saving graces that kept us married in spite of the tortuous road I attempted to navigate. We learned: "Whatever it is, it's something else."

So many times when we found ourselves about to get into an impasse because we disagreed about something, we'd pause, take a breath, look deeper and say, "What's really going on? Whatever it is, it's something else."

When we discovered this phrase, "Whatever it is, it's something else," just knowing we learned it, helped us avoid confrontations that may have erupted into disaster. Rather than fight, we plant a new idea.

Sow! We know "it ain't necessarily."

CHAPTER 26

THE PARENT TRAPEZE

"Becoming a father isn't difficult,
but it's very difficult to be a father."
Wilhelm Busch

It's not easy being a parent. It has similar perils to a flying trapeze act in a circus. Sometimes you're the catcher. You hang upside down, swinging back and forth and reach out to grasp desperate outstretched hands. Other times you're the leaper. At just the precise moment you let go of your safe swing, soar into the abyss, counting on someone to latch onto your grip. If you're working together it's an exciting show. It's hands holding hands. If not, disaster.

It takes a lot of practice to get the back and forth rhythm working just right. Trust becomes a dominant factor for all involved. But, how many times have I missed connections and come crashing down in disappointment or worse. It took me a long time to learn the painful lesson of how to reach out.

My father and I had a strained relationship. I know he loved me, because I was his son. I returned that love because the nuns who taught us our Catechism said the 4th Commandment to Honor Your Father and Your Mother made it mandatory. If not, I'd go to Hell. Who was I to challenge the good sisters, much less the word of God?

My father worked hard to provide a decent home for my mother, sister, brother and me. I was the youngest. He had a hard life growing up on a farm in Czechoslovakia. At age nine he took charge of the family farm when his father died from a kick in the head by a horse. With no role model it forced him to grow up fast on his own. He told me the story of how he spotted the branch of a tree with a slight curve. He cut the branch down and attached it to a wagon where he hooked up the horse. From stories like this and working beside him in construction I learned to become resourceful.

But, somehow as I got older we fell out of respect for one another. I know it happened in a gradual fashion. It may have started when I was about ten. For his birthday I wanted to surprise him with a sign I made in our woodworking shop in school. It was a simple wooden board with our address, 218, burned into it. The shop teacher helped me stain it and nail it to a stake to drive it into the ground. When I gave it to my father he held the sign by the stake and shook it like a tomahawk and laughed. Perhaps he meant it as a joke. But his antics crushed and

154

confused me. I became leery of wanting to be nice to him after that incident.

It wasn't all bad. One Christmas he got my brother Mike and me a train set. We loved it and played with it a lot. Another Christmas we got ice skates. But slow and steady, my father and I drifted apart. I'm sure he reached out to me when I wasn't prepared and I did the same to him with similar, unhappy results. Pretty soon the chasm got too great. We just could never reconcile our differences.

My pursuit of a theater career with so many disappointments baffled him. When Carol and I eloped it devastated him and my mother. Moving away from New Jersey to Maine only added to our family's separation, this time measured in hundreds of miles.

In an effort to make amends, my parents visited us in the new home I was building in Kennebunkport. Since my father worked as a brick mason when he was in construction, I asked him if he'd help me build front steps to the unfinished house. He agreed, and for that time we let the business of working together to solve the design, mixing cement and placing bricks to create the steps hide the strain between us.

In a few days we completed the steps with a small space for flowers. It looked pretty good. When we finished, my father looked tired and decided to take a nap. A short time later my mother came to me and said something was wrong with my father. He didn't feel good. He had chest pains. In one of the most important decisions I ever made, I called our local emergency department and they sent over their ambulance.

Their quick exam showed a serious problem with his heart. They took my father to the hospital in the next town. My mother and I followed. After checking my father's condition, the attending doctor told us my father had a heart attack. He'd need an operation and would have to regain his strength before they'd operate. So we took him home to rest.

In about a week my father got stronger and his doctor decided to operate. The operation was a success and the doctor gave him an excellent chance to make a recovery. He'd need more rest and care. The doctor told us travel would be dangerous, so we set up a room in our home. He and my mother stayed with us for several months.

During that time my brother Mike and his wife Lee and my sister Anne came to visit. Not quite the family reunion I had hoped for. My brother got mad at me because I dragged my father away to have a heart attack. My sister was more sympathetic and pitched in around the house. She even helped my daughter Gillian remove the lice in her hair that ran rampant through her third grade class. Not a lot of fun.

After my father had spent several months recuperating, the doctor gave permission for my parents to return to New Jersey. In spite of all we did to make amends, the strain remained. Several years later my father died of another heart attack. To this day I regret we never could find a way to heal our differences.

I didn't do much better with my mother. She was a very shy woman and the physical distance between Maine and New Jersey might as well have been between different solar systems. When my father died my mother went to live with my sister Anne and her family in Pennsylvania. After several years, she moved back to New Jersey to live with my brother Mike and his wife Lee. I will always be grateful for the loving care my sister and brother provided for my mother in her final years.

There's one relationship I had with my parents, sister and brother that made a curious and fun connection. My parents had two boys and a girl - my brother Mike and me and my sister Anne. Same pattern for my sister and her husband John: two boys and a girl - Stephen, Mark and Karen. My brother Mike and his wife Lee: two boys and a girl - Michael, Mark and Mary Ellen. My wife Carol and me: two boys and a girl – Josh, Noah and Gillian.

We all wondered if this family tradition of two boys and a girl would continue when my nieces and nephews married and started their families. But they had rebellions of their own and created a new pattern of siblings.

My sister's children: Stephen married RoxAnn. They have two girls and a boy – Tabatha, Stephanie and Nathan. Mark married Liz. They also have two girls and a boy - Alexandra, Gabriella and Nicholas. Karen has no children.

My brother's children: Michael married Andrea. They have three girls - Amy, Kelly and Lauren. Mark married Diane. They have two boys and four girls - Michael, Nicholas, Jessica, Tanya, Sarah and Elizabeth. Mary Ellen married Tom. They have two girls - Mary Beth and Kate Lynn.

More about Josh, Noah and Gillian in the next chapter.

Some children of children have married and now have children of their own. Don't worry. There won't be a quiz. I want to mention them because I'm very proud of all of them. In spite of the physical distances that separate us, when we get together for weddings and family events, it becomes a festive reunion.

While I regret I did not have a closer relationship with my parents, I do appreciate the many sacrifices they made for me. One of their gifts, which I still cherish, comes from our heritage. When my parents, sister and brother left Czechoslovakia to settle in Canada where I was born, they brought with them the Slovak language. When I was two years old we moved to New Jersey and lived near extended family and friends who shared our culture. I grew up with English as a foreign language. Whenever I did get together with my mother and father we always spoke in Slovak. At least we had that link to keep our tradition alive.

Now and then I'll meet someone from Eastern Europe and I always ask, "Rozumiz po Slovenski?" I wondered if we can share a conversation in Slovak. I don't get much of an opportunity to speak the language I grew up with, but it's a trip down a nostalgic lane when it happens.

CHAPTER 27

THE PARENT - THESIS

"A little learning is a dangerous thing."
Alexander Pope

"Lord, what fools these mortals be."
William Shakespeare

You might think all the strain I experienced with my father would have helped me be a better husband and father. As a parent I should have been able to write a thesis. (No doubt, to explain variations, subtleties and exceptions, it would include many parentheses.)

If only I had paid attention and made an effort to figure out where he and I went separate ways. Bullheaded, I focused on working hard to achieve my dream of a career in the theater, all the time hoping by some miracle I'd provide for the care and needs of my family. Instead, I missed out on the more important job of being there for them. Of course, I rationalized the time I devoted to "work" was for their benefit. But all my effort jumping from one dream to another turned out to be nightmares for them. All they saw was the struggle with no gainful result.

As we grew older and maybe even a little wiser, somehow we managed to get beyond my obsessions. Today we're close, stay in touch and care about what's happening to each other.

JOSHUA

When our first son Joshua was born in Washington, D.C. in 1965 I had just been fired from a construction job. I remember giving the clerk at the unemployment agency a cigar when I went to fill out papers to get benefits. He looked at the cigar, then at me, and said, "Good luck."

I had $10 in my pocket as I drove around the Capital looking for work. I passed a Salvation Army store and saw a rocking chair in the window. I thought this would make a perfect gift for Carol when she nursed Josh. I made a U-turn and went into the store. It looked in pretty good shape. It cost $7. I brought it home and Carol loved it. After all these years, we still have that chair.

Josh was the most loveable child. While he had a natural intelligence, for some reason he hated school. To this day he devours books. Ask him anything about the American Revolution or the Civil

War. He took the Mensa test for people with high IQs and passed.

Even early on he had a natural curiosity and quick wit. One day, Carol and I figured he and his brother Noah had reached the appropriate age to have a talk about the opposite sex. I didn't look forward to it, but went up to their room. As I entered I decided to just barrel ahead. I said, "Guys, I think it's time we had a conversation about sex."

Without skipping a beat, Josh said, "What do you want to know, Dad?"

That ended the conversation. I went downstairs and told Carol. We both had a good laugh.

Even with his reluctance to attend school, Josh graduated with high honors. He got accepted in the film department at the University of Bridgeport in Connecticut, but quit after one semester.

Like me, he went through a series of jobs. I'm sure some of his struggles came from seeing me change directions with disastrous results. Josh can be described as a guy with a big heart who likes to take care of other people. At a young age he took on odd jobs in an attempt to save us from the financial difficulties I managed to create.

With his friendly nature and determination, he found employment with a variety of companies. He worked at a radio station, a bank and had a management position in a car wash.

One day I visited Josh in the store where he sold athletic footwear. He happened to be waiting on an older man who had no idea about the new styles of sport shoes. I heard Josh describe how the inner soles had a special material to cushion the walk, how the tread of the soles made it more comfortable to walk and a variety of other technical features from the stitching, shoelaces and color combinations. Josh's knowledge of the shoes and his sincere manner convinced the man to buy the shoes.

After the sale I asked Josh how he knew so much about the shoes. He said, "Easy. I read all the literature about them."

He had an appreciation for auto racing and cars as a yongster. It seemed like a natural for him to form his own auto detailing company.

His ability to think fast combined with my inclination for show business gave us the idea to develop a television series about the cities in Maine. Our state has more than 30 locations with foreign names – like Paris, Norway, Mexico, Moscow, China and Denmark. He created the character Bruce McToose, The Intrepid Traveler. We taped shows where he went to Paris, Maine, looking for the Eiffel Tower and Norway, Maine, on a quest to see the famous fjords, among others. While in the town he'd meet local folks and learn the real history of each town. It would be like "Benny Hill meets National Geographic." We produced a short series and even got them aired on several television stations, including the Maine Public Broadcasting Network.

Like so many innovative projects, I couldn't get funding to continue and the series faltered. I still think it's a great idea.

Today Josh works in a key position for a company that shreds confidential documents. After an unsatisfactory marriage, he decided to live with us until he figures out his next move.

NOAH

Our second son, Noah, was born during a snow blizzard in Hackensack, New Jersey, in 1967. I drove through red lights on slippery roads to get Carol to the hospital in time.

Perhaps the storm served as a metaphor for a relationship that mirrored the strain between my father and me. Like Josh, Noah watched my struggles and I know it disillusioned him about my shortcomings as a provider.

He was such a beautiful child, but had several medical problems from the start. He would wake up crying and Carol and I took turns pacing the floor with him in an effort to ease his pain. After many sleepless nights, for him and us, we learned he had colic which medicine alleviated in a short time.

Noah also has a hip dislocation and had to wear a brace attached to special shoes to keep him from more injury. He was such a brave trooper about how he struggled to move around. To help him with his hip, Noah began dance lessons. He had an inspiring teacher and got to be very good. He pursued a professional dance career and performed in several major ballet companies, including those in Hartford, Connecticut and Louisville, Kentucky. But instead of helping, the dancing aggravated his hip, so he had to give it up.

Noah showed signs of brilliance by age two. He'd pick up a book and start to make out words. No doubt he got this ability from his mother, not me. Carol taught youngsters in several schools, including one in West Germany for children of military personnel.

Noah's love of learning and his high school grades earned him the salutatorian award. He gave an inspiring speech at his graduation. He won scholarships, but had difficulty finding himself as well as a productive career. He went through a tough period with me, traveled to California and wound up working at Walt Disney Studios. I think his going to California was not so much to go somewhere, but to get as far away from me as possible.

He has never stopped searching. If there's one trait we have in common, it's persistence. He demonstrated this quality in a most dramatic way.

During high school he was with a dance company that performed a variety of shows. He and three other youngsters did an exuberant tap dance number dressed as British Beefeaters with bright red uniforms, rifles and tall busy hats.

As the dance progressed, with each tap step, Noah's oversized hat began to slide down. Undaunted, he tapped away, keeping his cool as the hat began to slip lower and lower. Soon the hat slid over his eyes. While the other three dancers soldiered on, all eyes focused on Noah. A ripple of admiring laughter spread through the audience, wondering how Noah would finish. The dance ended with Noah keeping perfect time. His hat rested on his nose. The audience gave him a rousing cheer as he left the stage.

This type of determination led him to discover Hampshire College in Amherst, Massachusetts. The school has a reputation for encouraging students to create their own curriculum. A popular joke goes: Why did the Hampshire College student cross the road? Answer: To get three credits.

Noah majored in religious studies and talks about how he made a discovery while attending a lecture about anorexia. The speaker described the many young girls who deprived themselves of healthy food in order to stay thin. Since Noah didn't have an eating problem he internalized the message in an innovative way. Rather than starve themselves of food, do people starve themselves of success?

This discovery led him to write several books on the subject, among them *The Secret Code of Success.* Several of his books have been translated into foreign languages. Today he travels the world giving seminars about his discovery of "Afformations." Rather than make an affirmation like: I am rich or I am a success, Noah invites people to flip the idea and "form" it into a question. Such as: "Why am I a success?" "Why am I healthy?" "Why do I have loving relationships?" Such a question motivates finding the answer.

Noah has inspired thousands of people with his "Afformations" to change their lives and create sizeable incomes.

I can only guess, but I wonder if my struggles drove him to higher pursuits. To make his traveling easier he moved to central Ohio where he met and married a remarkable lady, Babette. Babette has a beautiful view of life and finds so many ways to find the best in people. She makes a wonderful compliment to Noah and his career, helping behind the scenes as well as appearing with him at speaking events. She is also very clever. Once, when Carol and I visited them, while Noah devoting time to his business, Babette and I converted a bookcase into a "secret" swinging door that led into another room. Not only is she a great partner for Noah, Babette makes a welcome addition to our family circle.

GILLIAN

Our daughter Gillian came as a wonderful surprise when we had settled in Maine. She was born in Biddeford in 1972. I gave her the middle name of "Joy" because she made us so happy.

Blessed with a winning personality, sunny smile and infectious laugh, Gillian lights up any room she enters. Filled with high energy and drive she worked several jobs through her high school years and would eventually have a successful career in radio sales and administration.

She attended Hollis College in Roanoke, Virginia, and transferred to the Franciscan University in Steubenville, Ohio. To complete her studies before she graduated she went to Europe as part of an exchange program.

She loved to do projects with me. We sewed a doll for Carol as a Christmas present, which still takes a place of honor among the decorations.

Once we had a water leak in the roof that created a dark stain down the wall of her room. She and I painted a tree over the stain with leaves, birds and a grassy background. She went to bed and woke up to a delightful summer scene even during some of our snowy, cold Maine winters.

During the winter a small pond across the street from our house froze. Gillian would drag me out with our skates and she became an eight-year-old

Sonja Henie. We'd create ice skating routines until the cold would force us back inside for warm drinks.

In a tribute to a music teacher who had an unfortunate accident, our school gave a program in his honor for the way he inspired his students. The program director asked Gillian and me to do a dance to "In the Mood." We practiced a jitterbug in our living room. When the time came for the performance we had it down pat. We ended up with me lifting Gillian on my shoulder as I spun around to the rhythm of the music. From the applause we got, I'd say we were a big hit.

A nearby hotel had a piano they didn't need. I got it for Josh who played the saxophone in the school band. I thought his musical talent would transfer to the piano. He took a couple of lessons but he didn't seem too interested. The piano sat against the wall waiting for someone to pay attention to it. One day Gillian walked up to the piano and, with one finger, figured out how to play the simple melody of "The Rose," the song made popular by Bette Midler.

From that moment she was entranced by the piano. She took lessons and over the years improved her skills and talent. After dinner she'd go to the piano and entertain us with Gershwin, the classics and songs she wrote herself. She produced two CDs and today plays special events.

She married a hard-working and caring man, Bruce, who grew up in the country setting of Fort

Kent, Maine. This has given him an appreciation of the outdoors. His "call of the wild" inspired me to climb Mount Katahdin, Maine's highest point, with him. They live in Lyme, New Hampshire, and have a son, Baxter, who gives Carol and me the thrill of being grandparents. When Baxter started speaking he called Carol "Gigi" and me "Peeka" because he had difficulty forming words at first. Now, at age seven, he has gained a wider vocabulary but still calls Carol "Gigi." I'm "Grandpa" and to Carol and me it's the sweetest sound he can make.

CAROL

Carol told me the story that explained why she put up with so many of my risky adventures. Her father wanted to start a pizza shop near their home in Bradford, Massachusetts. He was a good cook and resourceful. I'm sure he had the skills to make it a success. But, her mother, who lived up to her volatile Sicilian heritage, would not hear of it. Without his wife's support, Carol's father gave up the idea. Carol remembered how shattered he felt. That haunting memory prevented her from saying "No" when we started out together. But after a few too many of my disasters she learned how to express her own Sicilian temper. She was her mother's daughter.

Carol shared several career similarities with her older Louis (Lou) Dispenza. After Lou finished a tour of duty with the U.S. Army he and Carol commuted together to the teachers' college at Lowell

State College in Massachusetts a short distance from their home in Bradford. While Carol's original plan was to pursue a career in publishing, she found teaching youngsters gratifying.

Lou taught for five years at the Atkinson's Academy in neighboring New Hampshire and 42 years in Newburyport, Massachusetts. He also had a passion for the theater and with his wife – also named Carol – he started a community theater group in Georgetown in 1974. Although his wife passed away several years ago, Lou can look back on their participation in more than 100 productions as actors and behind the scenes.

Lou's daughter, Lorrie, from a previous marriage, was also bitten by the theater bug. She has a lovely singing voice, plays several musical instruments and has put her talents to good use in the theater group and other musical presentations.

There's no doubt in my mind that Carol's strength and belief in herself had a major positive impact on me, even though I often resisted it.

She provided the common sense and loving spirit that kept our family together through the desperate times I created. While I was oblivious, she was realistic. When I dreamed up a new scheme, she became practical. If I put us in jeopardy, she took steps to find a way to salvage us from disaster.

Once she took a teaching job to help with finances. She described a scene that still gives me chills when I think of it. As she drove to work in the early morning she would look back and see young Josh and Noah peering out the window with such sad looks on their faces. It broke her heart to leave the boys with a babysitter to care for them. But, she knew she had no other option at the time.

When the kids got older she worked in the high school library and took a part-time job she enjoyed in a bank. She had a great boss who appreciated her work and offered her a full-time position with better pay. As tempting as it was, she turned the job down because it would keep her away from the family.

Carol is a wonderful writer and has kept a personal journal since a young age. She saves her memories and creative ideas in hundreds of spiral-bound notebooks. Sometimes we have a different idea of an event that happened years ago. She'll tell me she has all the details logged in one of her notebooks. I learned there's no point to challenge her documentation of the facts. She's using her journal to write a memoir of her own.

With her confidence building and a passion for writing she decided to start a freelance writing business. She had a number of clients, but family matters interfered and she had to drop it.

For the sacrifices she made, for the dreams she put aside so I could follow mine, for her wisdom I too often rejected, for her patience which I stretched to the limit, for her guidance, care and love for our children, and me – for all this, and so much more, I can never praise or thank her enough. My life changed forever for the better when I met her. It took a while, but I finally got the clue.

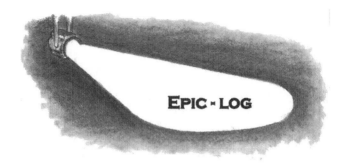

EPIC × LOG

"Oh, I'm a good old rebel, now that's just
what I am."
Innes Randolph

"Well, nobody's perfect!"
Final line from movie *Some Like It Hot*

Freddy, a co-worker and good friend had a sudden
heart attack while mowing his lawn. He was in his
mid-50s. He didn't survive.

Several years later I mowed my lawn on a
blistering hot July day. Although I had a self-
propelled push mower, the hilly ground of our
property made it tough going. Distracted by other
projects, I had let the grass grow taller than usual. So
both the mower and I struggled.

I had mowed non-stop for about an hour. My
T-shirt soaked through and sweat oozed down from

my forehead and burned into my eyes. Why I picked the hottest part of the day to mow is still a mystery. The muscles in my legs and arms ached as I maneuvered the mower around the flower beds. My breathing got heavier.

"Keep going, Steve," I told myself, "you're almost finished."

Then it happened. Out of nowhere. A gigantic BOOM!

It shook me. It stopped me cold. In spite of the heat a shiver went through my body. I looked around to see where the eerie noise came from. I didn't see anything. Then it hit me. I felt the sound more than heard it.

It was him. Freddy. I didn't see him. But I could sense his presence. At first I was puzzled and a little scared. It took a moment to collect myself. Then I got the clue. Freddy came to warn me. Without wasting another second I turned off the mower and shoved it into the garage. I staggered to the house and slumped onto the porch swing.

Freddy sat by my side. I let my breathing come easier. Freddy stayed with me until he was sure I was okay. Then, without a word he went away. Where? I have no idea. How he appeared is still beyond my understanding. But I know he came and I know why. He didn't want what happened to him to happen to me.

Carol had been watching me through the window. She was about to tell me to come inside and rest when she saw how much I struggled. She was surprised by my abrupt stop. When I told her about Freddy's strange appearance she understood. She knew about Freddy. I had often spoken of him and how he dedicated his life to his work. She knew about his tragic heart attack and what a great loss it was to all of us.

We learn about guardian angels as youngsters. Most of us grow out of that pleasant fantasy, until we need one. I couldn't be more pleased if Freddy made arrangements with whomever assigns guardian angels to pick me as someone to look after. He may have been watching over me from the beginning of my long bumpy journey. Time and space in that dimension have no limits. And, I proved beyond any doubt I could use all the help available.

In all I did I had the habit of pushing myself. Not just in a physical sense. I'd commit myself to every project with all my heart and soul. I'd get involved, lose track of time and everything around me. It meant I often went clueless about other, sometimes more important matters, like family and relationships.

No doubt it's the reason I became so obsessed with chasing a theater career. I believed if I worked hard enough, drove myself to the limit, followed every possible lead, how could I do anything but succeed? While all that chasing never got me a starring role or hit play on Broadway, something unexpected happened instead.

I realized my theater experiences created opportunities filled with a multitude of unintended consequences. They shaped my future work and career moves. I managed to find ways to use the creativity and ingenuity that mark the essence of crafting a theater piece. As a result I discovered a diverse number of opportunities in different parts of the country.

Strange as it seems, maybe Freddy or some other friendly guardian angel pointed me in a direction that suited me better.

Over the years I worked as an advertising manager, designed products and corrugated packaging, sold television commercials, owned my own ad agency, illustrated children's books and freelanced as an artist and writer. I also continue to teach writing and art classes. I even pumped gas on the night shift while I looked for more lucrative employment.

I worked with businesses that dealt in finance, health, industry, retail, publishing, trucking, real estate, vacation, construction and others. I created TV and radio commercials, publicity campaigns, print advertisements and literature.

One of my more elaborate promotions for the opening of a bank had me organize a parade with marching bands, horse riders, an American Revolutionary Militia battle and skydivers. Not quite a Michael Todd extravaganza, but not bad for a small Maine town.

As I mentioned earlier, the places I practiced these sundry crafts included New Jersey, Florida, Illinois, Washington, D.C, New York, Massachusetts and Maine. If I include working for the U.S Army as employment, I'd add Georgia, Maryland and South Korea to the list.

I'm pleased to say it wasn't all business.

On February 8, 2017 Carol and I celebrated our 52st anniversary. We point with pride to the wonderful people our two sons, Joshua and Noah, and our daughter Gillian have become. Now with a grandson, Baxter, we wallow in the joys of grandparenthood.

These fifty-two years had their share of frustrations, disappointments and sacrifices. As Winston Churchill once said, "If you're going through Hell, keep going." That's just what we did. We kept going.

Throughout all my rebellions, detours, speed bumps and hovering over the canyons, I recognize how the poignant memory of *South Pacific* shaped my life's decisions.

179

Was that experience a blessing or a curse? Do I thank Rodgers and Hammerstein or damn them? What would I have become without them?

The curtain hasn't lowered on my last act just yet.

I know myself well enough to say I haven't given up my search for more clues. Maybe, there's one waiting offstage, and I'll find the gumption to introduce another original rebellion.

AFTERWORD

In addition to writing, I am a freelance artist working in Pen & Ink, acrylics and pastel. Among my subjects are: homes and buildings, portraits, pets and equestrian art, sports, automobiles, maps, landscapes, cartoons and caricatures. I've also had the pleasure of illustrating several children's books.

Children's Books Illustrated by Steve Hrehovcik

- **"Murfy Finds A Home"**
  And
- **"Murfy's River Adventure"**
  Both Written by Robert Marier

  Both eBooks available at:
  Apple App Store; Google Play Appstore; Kobo Books; iBookstore

- **"The Power of Choice - The Greater Adventures of Humpty Dumpty"**
  Written by Joyce Guccione

- **"Julie's Climb"**
  Written by David Morse
  Available at: http://dmorseauthor.com

Be on the lookout for:
- My blog: **"I Learned It At The Movies"**

- A children's book:
  "The Bird Said to The Rabbit"

- A book of short stories - working title:
  "My God, What A Pleasant Surprise"

_____

- **"Rebel Without A Clue – A Way-Off Broadway Memoir"** is also an eBook

  Available at:
  Amazon; Smashwords; CreateSpace; iTunes
  Apple; Barnes & Noble; Kobo; Blio,
  Overdrive and Libraries

_____

You can also view examples of my art and writing on my website: www.kennebunkartstudio.com.

e-mail: steve@kennebunkartstudio.com